As one of the world's longest established and best-known travel brands, Thomas Cook are the experts in travel.

For more than 135 years our guidebooks have unlocked the secrets of destinations around the world, sharing with travellers a wealth of experience and a passion for travel.

Rely on Thomas Cook as your travelling companion on your next trip and benefit from our unique heritage.

Thomas Cook **traveller** guides

PROVENCE &
THE CÔTE D'AZUR

Roger Thomas

Your travelling companion since 1873

Written by Roger Thomas, updated by Anwer Bati
Original photography by Adrian Baker

Published by Thomas Cook Publishing
A division of Thomas Cook Tour Operations Limited.
Company registration no. 3772199 England
The Thomas Cook Business Park, 9 Coningsby Road,
Peterborough PE3 8SB, United Kingdom
E-mail: books@thomascook.com, Tel: + 44 (0) 1733 416477
www.thomascookpublishing.com

Produced by Cambridge Publishing Management Limited
Burr Elm Court, Main Street, Caldecote CB23 7NU

ISBN: 978-1-84848-231-9

© 2004, 2006, 2008 Thomas Cook Publishing
This fourth edition © 2010
Text © Thomas Cook Publishing
Maps © Thomas Cook Publishing/PCGraphics

Series Editor: Maisie Fitzpatrick
Production/DTP: Steven Collins

Printed and bound in Italy by Printer Trento

Cover photography: © Andreas Karelias/Alamy

Contents

Introduction

Provence and the Côte d'Azur are undoubtedly the most alluring part of France and also perhaps the most complex. Although the historical heart of Provence was small, the area known as Provence today comprises the Côte d'Azur, part of the Alps and through to parts of Languedoc.

Provence displays at least two incompatible personality traits. There is the pastoral face of Provence, a seductive visage of sleepy, golden-stoned farmhouses, vineyards and improbably blue skies.

Clashing with this bucolic vision is the Provence of the coast, a cosmopolitan – and often chaotic – mix of glamorous resorts and dense development, a victory of style over simplicity.

Further adding to the complex character of the area are its Alpine regions, where snowcapped peaks reach up into sunny skies; its high, empty plateaux, a no-man's-land between the Mediterranean and the Alps; its deep gorges like giant incisions in the earth's crust; its vast, lagoon-like flatlands along the Rhône delta; its retrospective qualities, embodied by an outstanding Roman heritage and idyllic medieval towns; and its dynamic, ever-onward economic impetus, driven by the high-tech Sun Belt industries of

this blessed, beautiful, blighted 'California of Europe'.

Provence can give you whatever you want. A hundred kilometres (60 miles) from the coast, you can sit in a café in a fountained medieval square and watch the world go by – which will probably consist of one man and his bicycle or *madame* doing the shopping.

An hour's drive away, you can rub shoulders with the seriously rich and famous on a jewelled coastal strip that is still *the* place to go and be seen, that still has the cachet and that still attracts yachts luxurious enough to rival the grandest of hotels.

THOMAS COOK'S PROVENCE

In 1871 Thomas Cook advertised the new destinations of Menton, Nice, Toulon and Marseille as part of the 'Winter Arrangements' for that year. By the 1880s, Cook's Christmas and New Year trips to the South of France were very popular with his middle- and upper-class customers.

Provence

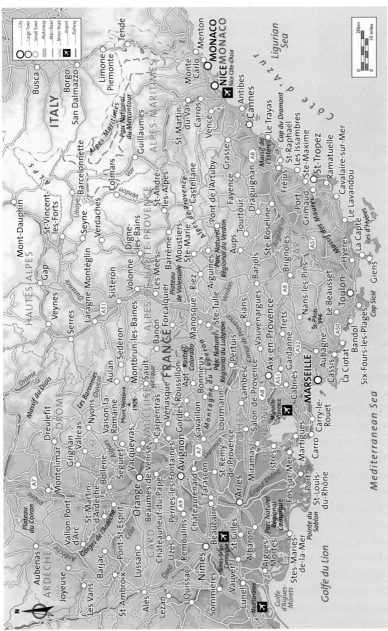

The land

Provence's boundaries embrace an amazing variety of scenery. Fertile valleys rise into rugged mountains, wooded hillsides and richly cultivated plains drift down to a palm-fringed, sandy coast. Towering crags and deep gorges in the Alpine country to the northeast contrast with the marshlands and long beaches of the Rhône delta to the southwest.

River and road

The fast-flowing Rhône has played a vital role in the development of trade. As well as defining Provence's western boundary, its broad valley is the region's crucial communications artery with the north, carrying the main road and rail links. Provence's other major river, the Durance, runs east to west, flowing into the Rhône south of Avignon.

Upland Provence

The mountain ranges striding across Provence are part of the geological upheaval that, over vast stretches of time, created the Alps. Mont Ventoux, the towering 1,909m (6,263ft) guardian of the northwestern approach to the region, has an overwhelming presence set off by vine-clad foothills. The northeastern gateway to Provence is through the mountains of the Alpes-de-Haute-Provence, a highland area unremittingly Alpine in character.

South-central Provence also has its uplands. The Luberon Mountains, although only half the height of Ventoux, are nonetheless a prominent upland barrier between the Plateau de Vaucluse and the coast. Winter sunshine along the Riviera highlights the proximity of the snowy peaks of the Alpes-Maritimes, only a short distance inland. You are never far away from hills and mountains in Provence: even the flat Rhône delta suddenly rises into the craggy Alpilles.

Gorges and sunken valleys

The limestone rocks of this region result in weirdly eroded mountain features (the Vaucluse's Dentelles de Montmirail are a classic – *see p35*). The rock also produces a near-subterranean spectacle where the limestone massifs have been intercut with deep gorges by the patient action of rivers. The most spectacular is the Grand Canyon du Verdon (*see pp128–9*), where the river snakes between cliffs almost 1km

(²/₃ mile) high. Along the coast west of Marseille, limestone valleys have sunk into the sea to produce a strange, fjord-like shoreline of deeply indented inlets known as *calanques* (*see p65*).

Climate

Generally speaking, Provence is a region of hot, dry summers and mild, sunny winters: a climate that continues to entice pleasure seekers as well as immigrants (usually from the grey northern latitudes), attracted as much by Provence's sunshine record as its new industries. The more northerly mountainous areas, however, are cooler and wetter in spring and autumn but provide ideal conditions for winter sports. Western parts of Provence are regularly exposed to the *mistral*, a penetrating north wind (*see box*). The hottest months are July and August, when temperatures soar to around 28°C (82°F) on average – and can get significantly higher – and rainfall is minimal, although thunderstorms are not uncommon. Some visitors prefer Provence in the spring, when the air is pleasantly warm and the countryside full of fresh, bright colours. Winters in the coastal region are mild, but autumn produces rain in October and November.

Economy

Despite massive tourism, agriculture remains an important part of the economy. Once-arid regions have long served as productive farmland thanks to centuries of irrigation, and Provence continues to produce more fruit and vegetables than any other part of France. Honey, herbs and fields of lavender are much in evidence. Perfume, oils and soaps, textiles, crystallised fruit, mines and salt beds reflect some of the traditional Provençal occupations. There is a significant wine industry, dominated by the Côtes du Rhône appellation. Much of Provence's industry is also concentrated in the Rhône Valley, and in recent years high-tech, scientific and communications industries have expanded considerably. The port of Marseille – one of the largest cities in France – is a busy commercial centre.

THE *MISTRAL*

The *mistral* has been known to drive man and beast mad. Suicide and murder rates are said to increase when this violent wind, which can reach speeds of 200km/h (124mph), whistles down the Rhône Valley for anything from three to ten days. Its name derives from the Provençal *mistrau*, meaning master.

When pressure is high over the mountains or low over the sea, the wind sweeps down from the Massif Central to the Mediterranean, gaining in force as it funnels through the Rhône Valley. In summer, you will need a sweater even on the sunniest day. In winter, the chill factor seems positively Siberian – which is why all wise Provençals have windowless north-facing walls. Provence's decorative wrought-iron bell towers – known as *campaniles* – are another testament to the power of the *mistral*: the wind rushes harmlessly through the ironwork cage instead of toppling a conventional stone spire.

History

Mesolithic times (Middle Stone Age)	Earliest known inhabitants.
6000 BC	Evidence of Neolithic (New Stone Age) pottery and agriculture.
Around 600 BC	Greek colonists found Massalia (Marseille).
600–100 BC	Greeks settle along the coast, leading to clashes with the local population. Greeks enlist the aid of their Roman allies.
150–50 BC	Romans advance into Provence.
58–52 BC	Conquest of Gaul by Julius Caesar. Southern Gaul becomes Provincia – 'the Province'.
46 BC	Roman amphitheatre is built at Arles.
19 BC	Construction of the Pont du Gard aqueduct near Nîmes.
1st century AD	Roman conquest of Provence completed early in the century.
2nd–3rd centuries AD	Roman influence at its height: roads and new towns built.
4th–5th centuries AD	Christianity grows in importance.
471	Arles invaded and taken by Visigoths, a western Germanic people.
476	The Roman Empire falls. Within 50 years, Provence is taken over by the Franks, another western Germanic people.
736–9	Saracens, nomadic Arabs from the deserts of Africa and the Middle East, invade southern France.
768–814	Charlemagne becomes king of the Franks and brings a semblance of order to Provence.
855	Provence is made a kingdom.
9th century	Continuing incursions by the Saracens.
1032	Provence becomes part of the Holy Roman Empire,

though the Counts of Provence retain their independence.

12th century	The Crusades lead to increasing prosperity along the coast.
12th–14th centuries	The era of the troubadours, poet-musicians whose major theme was courtly love.
1274	The papacy is given land – known as the Comtat Venaissin – in Provence. This influential episode paves the way for further papal links.
1309	The French Pope Clement V escapes political interferences in faction-ridden Rome by setting up court in Avignon.
1378–1417	The Great Schism of the Catholic Church, with one pope in Rome and the other in Avignon.
1409	The University at Aix-en-Provence is established.
1434–80	Provence flourishes under the enlightened Count René of Anjou (Good King René).
1486	Provence officially becomes part of France.
1539	The edict of Villers-Coterets declares French the official language of the region.
1545	Religious massacre in the Luberon Hills. Catholics and Protestants become embroiled in the Wars of Religion (1562–98).
1555	Nostradamus – physician, astrologer and citizen of Salon-de-Provence – publishes his predictions.
1580–95	Marseille becomes an important trading centre.
1720–22	The region is devastated by a terrible epidemic of the plague, killing 100,000 in two years.
1789–99	The French Revolution. Provence remains largely anti-revolutionary. However, in 1792, 500 revolutionary volunteers from Marseille parade in Paris to the Song of the Rhine Army. The song is rechristened *La Marseillaise* and becomes the French national anthem.

1793	The Siege of Toulon, during which the young Napoleon Bonaparte makes his mark. Within a decade Napoleon crowns himself emperor and proceeds to conquer much of Europe.
1814	Napoleon is forced by military defeat to abdicate and accept exile to the island of Elba.
1815	Napoleon returns from exile and marches on Paris through eastern Provence in his short-lived 'Hundred Days' of power, but is defeated at the Battle of Waterloo. His second exile is on the island of St Helena.
1860s	Casinos open at Monte-Carlo.
1914–18	World War I does not affect Provence territorially, though many of its men are killed in service.
1939–45	The Italians occupy Menton in 1940. Large-scale German occupation in 1942. Allied troops land on the Côte d'Azur in 1944. Germans remain in the mountains until 1945.
1945	Col de Tende is ceded from Italy to France.
1962	A new airport opens at Nice and soon becomes an international hub.
1970	Autoroute opens between Paris and Marseille.
1981	The high-speed TGV train links Paris with Marseille.
1993	The Grotte Cosquer is discovered, revealing paintings and a culture that date back over 25,000 years.
2001	TGV service continued to St-Raphaël and Nice.
2005	Prince Rainier III of Monaco dies and is succeeded by Prince Albert.
2007	Tram systems are opened in Nice and Marseille.
2009	80-year anniversary of the first Monaco Grand Prix.
2010	Fiftieth anniversary of the Juan-les-Pins Jazz Festival, which was the first in Europe.

Politics

Provence officially became a part of France in 1486, though this did not have much influence on the way of life because of the region's great distance from Paris, reinforced by Provence's ancient ties with Italy. But the coming of the railways in the 19th century changed everything. Not only was the local Provençal language undermined by French, but the region attracted tourists who created along the coast a cosmopolitan and wealthy society far removed in its values and lifestyle from the traditional countryfolk of the region.

It is this pattern that produced the extremes of right-wing power in the larger regional cities such as Nice and Cannes, and the contrasting socialist or communist strongholds inland. But even among the cities, there are exceptions to the rule.

The biggest city in Provence is Marseille. It has for many years been socialist (notwithstanding a worrying far-right enclave, which has grown significantly in recent elections) with a suspicion of central government. Nice, on the other hand, has an unequivocally right-wing tradition. The city was ruled by a single family for many decades, and its reign ended only when charges of large-scale corruption were levied against the Mayor who, consequently, fled France.

When Algeria gained independence from France in the late 1950s, Provence became home for hundreds of thousands of *pieds noirs*, the French settlers who fled back to the mother country. Over the years these settlers have become a defined political force, and it seems probable that the presence of this uprooted community has accounted for the high level of support for the ultra-right-wing National Front in cities such as Toulon and Nice as well as in smaller places like Aubagne. Right-wing opinion is further fuelled by what is increasingly being perceived as a problem with North African immigrants and other 'foreigners'.

In the 1980s Jean-Marie Le Pen's National Front party started to gain a foothold in the south. Le Pen's party saw a continuing rise in popularity during the 1990s but fell back after Le Pen was outvoted for France's presidency in 2002 by Jacques Chirac. He failed once more in 2007, when the centre-right Nicolas Sarkozy was elected.

As a whole, Provence forms part of the Provence-Alpes-Côte d'Azur regional government, which is controlled by a left-wing coalition.

Culture

The culture of Provence finds expression everywhere: not just in artistic events, but in the way people live and in the traditions they have inherited. In ancient times the region was a staging post between the Mediterranean to the south and Gaul to the north. The resulting cross-fertilisation of cultures has produced a unique mix.

Generalisation is a notorious activity. There will always be those who claim that the worldly inhabitants of Aix or Avignon harbour pretensions of sophistication unknown to the humble Provençal peasant (if such a person exists any longer). Nonetheless, it is reasonable to claim that Provençals are a proud and independent people who, though wary and to some degree suspicious of strangers, can be hospitable and generous to a fault once their trust has been earned. They have a dialectical language of their own, Provençal, which, although not commonly spoken today, is still taught as an option in most schools. It differs in many respects from classical French and is distinguished by the richness of its vowels (*see p20*).

Festivals and fêtes

The pastoral tradition remains strong in Provence. The French in general have an

Water jousting in the Camargue

almost mystical relationship with the land. Many city dwellers are today's representatives of families who, until relatively recently, lived a rural existence. Although the most modern of industries are nowadays to be found in Provence, the locals pride themselves on their deep attachment to the land. For them it is also a matter of continuity, seen in their reverence for traditions, many of which are rooted in rural antiquity.

Beehive-like *bories* near Gordes

Some of the festivals and fêtes with which the region abounds celebrate the harvesting of crops and the generosity of nature. Flower parades and wine festivals add zest and colour to the life of many a town and village; special events mark the custom of transhumance (the migration of sheep and cattle from winter plain to summer pasture), while fishermen's festivals are evidence of the importance of the sea. Adept though the early Christians were at giving new meaning to old customs, distinctly pagan undertones linger on in some of these local festivals.

Rural festivals flourish alongside more sophisticated occasions such as the Cannes Film Festival (*see pp96–7*) and musical events of various kinds. Sophisticates can enjoy everything from opera to jazz, for instance, at summer festivals in Arles and Avignon.

Architecture

Visitors with an eye for architecture will find much to delight them in Provence. The region's Roman remains are among the finest to be seen anywhere, and richly decorated medieval churches demonstrate the degree of spiritual and material wealth the people have invested in their religious life. Romanesque chapels and wayside shrines add to the region's diversity. Among Provence's most distinctive features are the dry-stone beehive huts known as *bories*, originally the work of semi-nomadic shepherds; the best examples are in the Luberon.

Crafts old and new

The earliest inhabitants of Provence, although belonging to a hunting and fishing culture, were by no means uncivilised. The necklaces of fishbone found on prehistoric skeletons uncovered here prove their manual dexterity and aesthetic sense.

Artistry of a different kind flourishes in Provence today, a region famous for the quality of its craftwork. From the religious figurines known as *santons* (*see p125*) to the blown-glass bubbles of Biot, Provence has a wealth of beautiful objects to tempt the discriminating visitor. It is not difficult to discern a continuity at work here, typified by the way old blends with new in this heritage-conscious part of France.

Festivals

Festivals and fêtes are a way of life in Provence. They range from small, informal village gatherings to prestigious international events, and embrace all aspects of life. They celebrate lavender and lemons, cinema and theatre, religion and the rice harvest, opera and jazz, wine and food. Apart from the Cannes Film Festival, the main event of the year is Avignon's eclectic summer Festival of Dramatic Art. Aix-en-Provence's Festival of Art and Music is also particularly important.

The village festivals are great fun. Anyone can take part for the price of an all-inclusive ticket. Ask at local tourist offices for details.

The Gypsy Festival

In May each year, gypsies from all over Europe head to Stes-Maries-de-la-Mer, a custom that dates at least to the 16th century. Their pilgrimage hinges on the figures of Sarah and the three Marys – Mary Magdalen, Mary Salomé and Mary Jacobé, who supposedly arrived here from the Holy Land. The group's servant, Sarah, became the gypsies' patron saint. The festival is an animated occasion.

January

Cannes
Shopping Festival.
www.cannesshoppingfestival.com
Monaco
Monte Carlo Rally.
www.acm.mc
www.montecarlofestivals.com

February

Menton
International Lemon Festival.
Tel: 04 92 41 76 76.
www.feteducitron.com
Nice
Carnival and Battle of Flowers.
Tel: 08 92 70 74 07.
www.nicecarnaval.com

April

Monaco
Monte Carlo Spring Arts Festival (runs until May).
Tel: (337) 92 16 22 99.
www.printempsdesarts.com

May

Cannes
International Film Festival.
Tel: 04 92 99 84 22.
www.festival-cannes.fr
Grasse
Rose Festival. *www.ville-grasse.fr*
Nice
Fête de Mai. *www.nicetourisme.com*

St-Tropez
Les Bravades de St-Tropez. Three-day folk festival. *www.ot-saint-tropez.com*
Stes-Maries-de-la-Mer
24–25 May. Gypsy pilgrimage. *Tel: 04 90 97 82 55.*
Toulon
Festival of Music. *Tel: 04 94 18 53 00.*

June
La Ciotat
Festival of Cinema. *Tel: 04 42 08 61 32. www.tourisme-laciotat.com*
Menton
Month of Gardens. *www.menton.fr*
Tarascon
Tarasque Festival. *Tel: 04 90 91 03 52.*

July
Aix-en-Provence
Festival of Art and Music.
Festival of Dance. *Tel: 04 42 17 34 34. www.festival-aix.com*
Arles
Photographic Festival. *Tel: 04 90 96 76 06. www.rencontres-arles.com*
Avignon
Festival of Dramatic Art (runs until August). *Tel: 04 90 27 66 50. www.festival-avignon.com*
Carpentras
Les Estivales (runs until August). *Tel: 04 90 63 00 78.*
Hyères
Festival of Jazz. *Tel: 04 94 01 84 50.*
Juan-les-Pins
Jazz Festival. *Tel: 04 92 90 53 00.*
Manosque
Festival of Jazz. *Tel: 04 92 76 16 00.*

Nice
Jazz Festival. Mid-July in the Roman amphitheatre at Cimiez. For tickets *tel: 0892 70 75 07. www.nicejazzfestival.fr*
Orange
Chorégies d'Orange (festival of opera and classical music). *Tel: 04 90 34 24 24.*
St-Rémy-de-Provence
Organa Festival (organ music). *Tel: 04 90 92 05 22.*
Vaison-la-Romaine
Festival of Music, Theatre and Dance (runs until August). *Tel: 04 90 36 02 11.*
Vence
Les Nuits du Sud. Month-long outdoor world music festival. *www.ville-vence.fr*

August
Châteauneuf-du-Pape
First weekend in August: *Fête de la Véraison. Tel: 04 90 83 71 08.*
Malaucène
Summer Festival at the beginning of August. *Tel: 04 90 65 22 59.*
Salon-de-Provence
Festival International de Musique. Tel: 04 90 44 82 90.

September
Arles
Festival of the Rice Harvest. *Tel: 04 90 18 41 20.*
Cassis
Festival of Wine. *Tel: 04 42 01 71 17.*

December
Marseille
Santons Fair (runs until January). *Tel: 04 91 13 89 00.*

Impressions

Provence offers a variety of different experiences for visitors: some prefer the lush vineyards of the Vaucluse, others the more barren high country of the Var or the mountains of the Alpes-de-Haute-Provence. The glamour and glitz of Cannes and St-Tropez cast an irresistible spell over many, while others prefer the uncomplicated appeal of family resorts such as La Ciotat or the natural wonders of the Camargue.

Finding your way around

This book is subdivided into the region's five *départements* – Vaucluse, Bouches-du-Rhône, Var, Alpes-Maritimes and Alpes-de-Haute-Provence. If each *département* were a self-contained entity with its own unique, distinct set of scenic characteristics, then the task of explaining 'what is where' in Provence would be a simple one. But Provence is not that tidily arranged. The classic violator of departmental borders is the Côte d'Azur, the 'azure-blue coastline'. We have all heard of it, but where exactly is it? Theoretically it stretches from St-Raphaël (in the Var), along the coast of the Alpes-Maritimes, through the independent Principality of Monaco to the Italian border. In practice, the Côte d'Azur label is often applied to the entire French Riviera as far west as Cassis (in the Bouches-du-Rhône).

Similarly, major landscape features such as the Montagne du Luberon and the Alpine Parc National du Mercantour span departmental boundaries. Overlap also applies to the precise definition of Provence itself. Within the context of this book, Nîmes, Pont du Gard and the western Camargue are all included within the Bouches-du-Rhône section, even though this is not strictly correct (these places are in the *département* of the Gard).

Cities and coastal resorts

Provence, for all its natural beauty, also boasts big cities and busy resorts. The cities vary from stylish Aix to sprawling Marseille, slightly dowdy Arles to self-confident Avignon. The resorts, too, have distinct characters. A coastal strip that seems on first impressions to be a continuous, unbroken development reveals undeniable differences on closer examination.

The old maxim 'Cannes is for living, Monte Carlo for gambling and Menton for dying' still has a ring of truth. Nice

PERCHED VILLAGES OF PROVENCE

'A village stands on high ground, partly as a defence against the Saracens, but mainly for the good view . . . The peasants, who know how to enjoy life, take time to look at things.' These were the words of Provençal writer Jean Giono (1895–1970).

The 'perched villages' (*villages perchés*) of Provence were built for security in troubled medieval times. Built in dense clusters that took maximum advantage of steep slopes and heights, the villages almost merge into their surroundings. However, very few proved to be impregnable.

By the start of the last century many were in a sorry state, the locals understandably preferring life in newer houses with modern conveniences.

Today the immaculately renovated villages – many with shops, artisans' quarters and exclusive restaurants – make every attempt to attract rather than repel visitors.

and St-Tropez, the other really famous places along the coast, have similarly strong – and surprising – personalities: surprising because of the vastness of Nice (which is more city than resort) and the smallness of world-famous St-Tropez.

Resorts such as Hyères and Ste-Maxime manage to preserve a sense of dignity on an intensely developed, over-exploited coast, which unfortunately shows all the signs of overheating (in the non-climatic sense). Yet there are still areas of relative wilderness: the indented coast between Marseille and Cassis, the lovely Îles d'Hyères and, to a lesser extent, the mountain-backed shorelines fringing the Massif des Maures and Massif de l'Esterel.

In the country

Provence's landscapes range from sunny valleys to snowy peaks. The characteristic Provençal scene – the golden-stoned farmhouse set among sun-baked vineyards – is most readily found in the Vaucluse or Bouches-du-Rhône regions. The higher country of the Vaucluse Plateau and the Var offers huge, open spaces that reveal a hint of Alpine influence. The Alps themselves lie further north and east, in the thinly populated upper reaches of the Alpes-de-Haute-Provence and the Alpes-Maritimes.

Customs and lifestyle

Provence is a land where undue haste is not considered a virtue. Its people are far from indolent, but they instinctively believe that quality of life is much more important than intensity of activity. Even in the busiest cities such as Marseille, time is found for a leisurely lunch.

To understand the character of the Provençals, one must appreciate that from time immemorial their lives have been shaped by the slow turn of the seasons. They are essentially a rural people with respect for the land, and this respect applies even to city folk, whose gardens are often small islands of perfection. Their natural reserve quickly gives way to open-handed generosity when they feel you are to be trusted, and their laughter and high spirits are infectious.

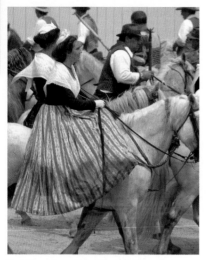

Traditional Provençal women 'cowboys'

A hint of formality

The sense of being part of an old civilisation where the values of yesteryear are not easily discarded is confirmed by the etiquette of the region. Women are still greeted in the customary way with two or three kisses on the cheek (among men, even close friends observe a quick handshake), but this does not imply any taking of liberties. Manners tend to be far more formal than in Britain, for example, and the tourist would be well advised to address people as *monsieur, madame* or *mademoiselle.*

It also pays to know a little French, for an attempt to speak the language, however imperfectly, is regarded as an act of courtesy to the host country. Remember, too, that people living in the Provençal countryside are much more conservative than city dwellers in their attitude to dress. Topless bathing is perfectly acceptable on the beaches, but walking around town in beachwear is not. It is also a breach of propriety to enter a church or cathedral while scantily dressed.

Traditional costume

Tradition plays a large part in the life of Provence. The traditional costumes worn by many families during the numerous festivals bring a distinctive feel to life in the region. Christmas and Easter have their own special rituals, which are still faithfully observed.

A social dimension to food

Food, of course, is more than mere sustenance to the Provençals. Their insistence on quality reflects an attitude to food – found throughout France, in fact – that has profound social, even artistic, dimensions.

Calorie-conscious tourists may view such delights with trepidation, deciding perhaps that some of the salads served as separate courses are meals in

OPENING TIMES

Most religious sites are open at all reasonable times, though sightseeing visits should always take place when church services are not being held. Other sites often close in winter or have very restricted opening hours. Even in summer, many (especially museums) are closed at some time during the week, normally on Monday or Tuesday. Specific details are given for each site mentioned; in general, all main sites are freely accessible and open daily during the tourist season.

themselves. What they should not deny themselves is the experience, for in Provence meals are social occasions to be enjoyed to the full.

Café society also flourishes here, and not only among the wealthier classes. Enjoying a *pastis* or *café crème* after a wander round the market is something that practically everyone does on a regular basis. It is part of the unhurried *vie provençale* (Provençal way of life).

In day-to-day matters old customs die hard. Shopping is less a chore than a social activity that gives savour to life. Open-air markets not only offer goods

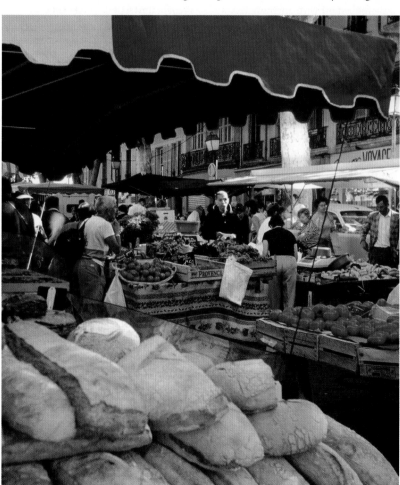

The market stands at the hub of village and town life

and produce of all kinds, they also bring a town or village together once a week. These markets serve as a natural interface between locals and visitors to the region. To outsiders, they reveal how carefully the Provençals select the items that make up their everyday meals. These are folk not easily fobbed off with anything less than the best, for it seems that nature has equipped them with antennae highly sensitive to the shoddy and second-rate, enabling them to maintain high standards in a rapidly changing world.

Language

Provençals are justly proud of the fact that their language continues to exist despite all the pressures exerted by mass communications and the cultural dominance of French. The official language of the region is, of course, French, but Provençal – the tongue of the medieval troubadours – still survives. Not that you are likely to hear it being spoken in the streets. Provençal today lives on as a literary language studied at school or university, and also – more visibly – on bilingual place-name signs.

Provençal is derived from the vulgar Latin that entered the region with Roman colonisation. It is a dialect of the southern Languedoc (the *langue d'oc* as opposed to the *langue d'oïl* of northern France, *oc* and *oïl* meaning 'yes' in the south and north respectively). Its written form reaches back ten centuries, for around the year 1000 Provençal became the language of courtly poetry. Although gradually superseded by French as a written language, it survived as a spoken tongue until relatively recent times.

Provençal differs from French in the openness of its vowels. In standard French, unstressed vowels tend to contract or to disappear altogether, but in Provençal they are distinctly voiced. This makes for a rounder, more musical language, which in many respects is closely related to Catalan.

Optional lessons

A new awareness of the language arose in the first half of the 19th century, when the poet Frédéric Mistral helped found the Félibrige movement, which aimed to restore the Provençal language and codify its spellings. But revival proved a forlorn hope, and by the time Mistral received the Nobel Prize in 1904, Provençal had already given way to French as the tongue in everyday use.

Today the language is taught as an option in most schools, and there is a faculty of Provençal language and literature at the University of Aix-en-Provence. Its official encouragement should ensure its survival. It would take a brave – or foolhardy – person today to echo the sentiments of 19th-century tourist Lady Hester Stanhope who, in 1846, dared to pronounce it 'a most disagreeable jargon'!

olives vertes
à l'ail et au
basilic

olives noires
pimentées
0,80 €

Olives play a vital role in the Provence economy

Vaucluse

Vineyards, lavender fields and craggy hills cover this département, *a beautiful area that lies under the watchful gaze of Mont Ventoux. The Vaucluse's western boundary is defined by the wide valley of the Rhône. Eastwards, the rich Côtes-du-Rhône vineyards rise into a roller-coaster landscape of green hills and valleys spread beneath the bare-topped heights of Mont Ventoux.*

Apt

This town, which spreads itself out across a wide valley on the northern approach to the Luberon Mountains, is more noteworthy for its location than its inherent charm. It is, however, well known for its associations with a number of edible things. Foremost

Vaucluse

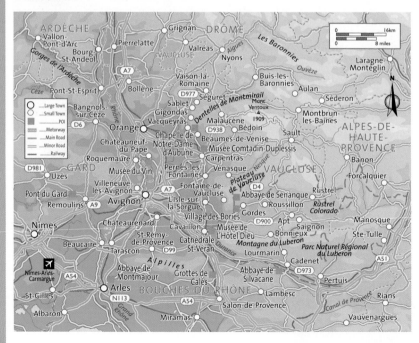

among these are speciality chocolates and candied fruit; and Apt is the centre of the truffle trade in winter.

There are a number of sweet manufacturers in Apt, some of whom specialise in glacéed or crystallised fruits – cherries, plums, pears, apricots, pineapples, etc. These and many more confections are on sale at the Saturday market, along with a magnificent array of local produce. The market, in the rue des Marchands, is a social as well as a shopping experience. Cars make way for stallholders, musicians, jugglers and craftspeople. Apt also has another, smaller 'farmers' market' on Tuesday morning (April to December) at cours Lauze de Perret.

Although the approach to the town is undistinguished, there are many interesting and attractive corners to explore. But most visitors inevitably look further afield, for the town is an excellent base for exploring the **Parc Naturel Régional du Luberon** (*see pp24–5*).

Ancienne Cathédrale Ste-Anne

This 11th-century building in the centre of town, dedicated to the mother of the Virgin Mary, also shows evidence of an earlier religious settlement in its two ancient crypts (Romanesque and pre-Romanesque).

Maison du Parc Naturel Régional du Luberon (Luberon Regional Natural Park Office)

The visitor centre, in an attractive 17th-century mansion, has a wide range of information on the park, the flora and fauna of the region, and a palaeontology museum.

60 place Jean-Jaurès. Tel: 04 90 04 42 00. www.parcduluberon.fr. Open: Mon–Fri 8.30am–noon & 1.30–6pm. Closed: Sat & Sun.

Musée de l'Aventure Industrielle

Opened in 2003, the museum showcases Apt's traditional industries: ceramics, preserved fruits and ochre.

14 place du Postel. Tel: 04 90 74 95 30. Open: Oct–Jun Wed–Sat 10am–noon & 2–5.30pm; Jul–Sept Mon–Sat 10am–noon, 3–6.30pm, Sun 3–7pm. Admission charge.

Musée d'Histoire et d'Archéologique

Exhibits cover prehistory, the Gallo-Roman period (Apt was a prosperous Roman colony), and ceramics from the 17th to 19th centuries.

Rue de l'Amphithéâtre. Tel: 04 90 74 95 30. Open: by appointment only for group guided tours. Admission charge.

Rows of lavender bushes are a common sight

Tour: The Luberon

The Parc Naturel Régional du Luberon takes in two départements – the Vaucluse and Alpes-de-Haute-Provence (see pp136–7 for details). This tour concentrates on the western part of the park.

The tour, which at a leisurely pace could take all day, begins at Apt, the region's major town and location of the visitor centre for the park (see p22).

Take the D48 southeast to the perched village of Saignon and its Romanesque church. The D232 and D113 lead southwest to Buoux and the Fort de Buoux.

1 Fort de Buoux

This is an abandoned fortified village standing on a natural platform and accessible by foot. The bastions, ramparts, keep, rock dwellings, 13th-century church and remains of a recently excavated medieval village can all be seen.
Follow the D943 south through the Combe de Lourmarin, the only road to cut through the Luberon Mountains, for 20km (12 miles), to Lourmarin.

2 Lourmarin

Writers Henri Bosco and Albert Camus both lived in this attractive village, which is guarded by a Renaissance château (guided tours available, tel: 04 90 68 15 23). From here you can take a short detour further south to visit the Abbaye de Silvacane (*see p48*).

From Lourmarin, return along the D943, turning left along the D36 to Bonnieux.

3 Bonnieux

The bucolic picture of Provence created by Peter Mayle, undoubtedly the Luberon's best-known contemporary English writer, is not, of course, wholly accurate. Bonnieux, Lacoste and Ménerbes are fashionable places that combine sophistication with a certain down-to-earth charm. Bonnieux is a lively, attractive, terraced village situated on a steep hill commanding wonderful views across to Lacoste, Gordes, the Vaucluse Plateau and Mont Ventoux. Its **Musée de la Boulangerie** (Museum of Baking, *tel: 04 90 75 88 34; open: Wed–Mon 10am–12.30pm & 3–6pm – check for winter times; admission charge*), an ancient bakery, is worth a visit.
Take the D3/D109 to Lacoste.

4 Lacoste

Lacoste is famous – or, more accurately, infamous – for its château, home of

Donatien Alphonse François, better known as the Marquis de Sade (1740–1814). Take the D103 to Ménerbes, passing the **Ancienne Abbaye St-Hilaire**, a 12th-century religious site with a surviving chapel. Ménerbes was the scene of a long siege in the 16th-century Wars of Religion, when it was a Protestant stronghold. Its ancient fortifications are now largely in ruins.

From Ménerbes take the D188 to Oppède-le-Vieux.

5 Oppède-le-Vieux

Oppède towers over a wild landscape of rocks and woodland. Once abandoned, it has been sympathetically restored and given a new role as an arts and cultural centre.

The D176 leads to the village of Maubec and on to the D2. Cross the D900, staying on the D2 for Gordes (see pp36–7).

Continue east on the D2, turning right on the D102 for Roussillon (see pp39–40). Return to Apt via the D4/D900.

Tour: The Luberon

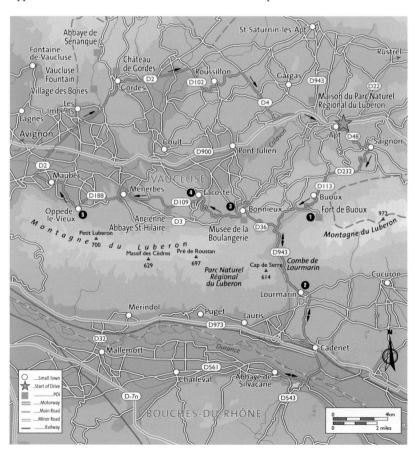

Avignon

The historic, stylish city of Avignon stands alongside the curving Rhône on a wide, flat valley. It is the largest and most important city in the Vaucluse. Visitors approaching the city might begin to suspect that Avignon does not live up to expectations. Fear not: the historic heart of the city will not disappoint. Persevere through the bland suburbs to the ring of city walls, still complete, that encloses the Avignon of the guidebooks.

The walls, still defended by 39 towers, date from medieval times. Avignon's history can be traced as far back as the Bronze Age, though it was in the 14th century that it became the city of the Popes. In 1309 Pope Clement V sought refuge here from the factionalism of Rome, establishing an administrative base that eventually rivalled the Vatican. The glory of the imperial Palais des Papes (Palace of the Popes) confirms Avignon's medieval status.

The city is today a major artistic centre with a prestigious summer festival, focused largely on theatre and film. Across the river stands Avignon's sister city, **Villeneuve-lès-Avignon**.

Cathédrale Notre-Dame-des-Doms

This 12th-century Romanesque church holds the tombs of two pontiffs.
Place du Palais. Tel: 04 90 86 81 01.
Open: daily 8am–6pm.

Musée Angladon

Based on the collection of couturier Jacques Doucet (1853–1929), this privately run museum houses (among other things) a small but fine collection of impressionist art, and the only Van Gogh still permanently in Provence. It also stages excellent temporary exhibitions.
5 rue Laboureur. Tel: 04 90 82 29 03.
www.angladon.com. Open: summer Tue–Sun 1–6pm; winter Wed–Sun 1–6pm. Admission charge.

Musée Calvet

A fine 18th-century mansion that contains classical and modern paintings, wrought-iron pieces, Greek sculpture and exhibits of local prehistory bequeathed by Dr Esprit Calvet to his native town.
65 rue Joseph-Vernet. Tel: 04 90 86 33 84. Open: summer Wed–Mon 10am–6pm; winter Wed–Mon 10am–1pm & 2–6pm. Admission charge.

Carved doors, Church of St Pierre, Avignon

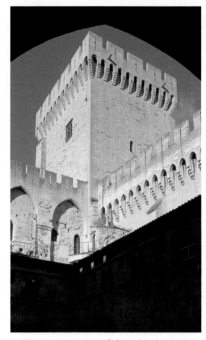

Looking up to a tower of the Palais des Papes

Musée du Petit Palais

The museum, based at the episcopal palace acquired by the papacy in 1335, contains a huge collection of paintings and sculptures, mostly Italian, from the 13th to 15th centuries.
Place du Palais. Tel: 04 90 86 44 58. Open: summer Wed–Mon 10am–1pm & 2–6pm; winter Wed–Mon 9.30am–1pm & 2–5.30pm. Admission charge.

Palais des Papes

This majestic palace, with its soaring architecture, was built in the 14th century as a fortress-cum-palace to serve as a French base for the popes. Its battlements and towers are impressive.

Within the walls, the vast dimensions are even more evident – especially the 48m (157ft) long Grand Tinel (Banqueting Hall) and Grande Audience (Great Audience Chamber). The palace is an overlap of two styles, reflecting the personalities of two popes, Benoit XII and Clement VI. The first palace is sober, even austere, while the second is an opulent homage to an all-powerful prelate. During the French Revolution the Palais was ransacked and first turned into a prison, then a barracks, which it remained until the early 20th century.
Place du Palais. Tel: 04 90 27 50 00. www.palais-des-papes.com. Open: 1–14 Mar daily 9am–6.30pm; 15 Mar–30 Jun & 16 Sept–1 Nov daily 9am–7pm; Jul & 1–15 Sept daily 9am–8pm; Aug daily 9am–9pm; Nov daily 9am–5.45pm. Closed: Dec–Feb. Last admission one hour before closing. Admission charge.

Pont St-Bénézet

This famous landmark is celebrated by the ubiquitous folk song *Sur le pont d'Avignon*. The bridge itself comes as something of an anticlimax, for it no longer crosses the river. The stunted structure, once 900m (2,953ft) long, was largely washed away in a 17th-century flood. Nevertheless, a walk along what is left of the narrow bridge is a ritual for all visitors to Avignon.
Tel: 04 90 85 60 16. Open: as for Palais des Papes. Admission charge.

Walk: Avignon

Avignon's main places of interest are easily visited on foot, for they are contained within the walls running around the city centre. If you are arriving by car, use one of the car parks located alongside the walls. Pedestrianised shopping streets lead off from the rue de la République, the main thoroughfare.

Allow at least half a day for the walk, with extra time for a full visit to the Palais des Papes.

From the Office de Tourisme at 41 cours Jean-Jaurès (tel: 04 32 74 32 74) walk along rue Joseph Vernet.

1 Rue Joseph-Vernet

This street is one of the most elegant in Avignon, with expensive shops selling *haute couture* and high-class confectionery. The Musée Calvet and the Musée Requien (a natural history museum dedicated to Esprit Requien, a 19th-century naturalist, closed Tue and Sun) are located side by side.
Continue along rue Joseph-Vernet towards place Crillon.

2 Place Crillon

Place Crillon's furniture shops sell exclusive pieces. Porte de l'Oulle, a gateway in the town walls, leads to the main road bridge over the Rhône.
At the far end of rue Joseph-Vernet, turn right, then first right into rue Petite Fusterie (the antique dealers' quarter), then turn left into rue St-Agricol.

3 Église St-Agricol

Église St-Agricol is located along the street of the same name. Dating from the 14th to 16th centuries, it is dedicated to Avignon's patron saint. It is one of the city's best Gothic edifices, with a beautifully carved 15th-century façade and fine medieval works of art.
Continue on to the Palais du Roure on rue Collège du Roure at the bottom of the place de l'Horloge.

4 Palais du Roure

The 15th-century Palais du Roure houses a cultural centre for Provençal studies and a museum of popular art and traditions (open to the public Tue at 3pm, or on request, *tel: 04 90 80 80 88*). Avignon's café society congregates along the place de l'Horloge, a wide, open space full of brasseries and flanked by the City Hall and Opera House.
Rue Villar leads to an even more impressive open space, the place du Palais at the foot of the mighty Palais des Papes (Palace of the Popes) and Cathédrale

Notre-Dame-des-Doms. At the far end of the square is the Musée du Petit Palais. From here, little alleyways lead to the famous pont St-Bénézet (signposted). From the bridge, walk alongside the ramparts to the flights of steps that zigzag up the cliff face to the beautiful gardens of Rocher des Doms.

5 Jardins Rocher des Doms

These restful gardens, set on a high outcrop overlooking Avignon and neighbouring Villeneuve-lès-Avignon, command wonderful views northwards across the majestic Rhône. This is the perfect place for a picnic.

Take the Escaliers Ste-Anne (the steps down from the gardens) to rue Banasterie.

6 Chapelle des Pénitents Noirs

Detour north along rue Banasterie for the Chapelle des Pénitents Noirs, an 18th-century Baroque edifice. Southbound, rue Banasterie leads to place St-Pierre and its church (14th to 16th centuries), noted for its flamboyant Gothic-style façade. Follow rue des Fourbisseurs to place St-Didier, which also has a fine Renaissance church.

Rue Laboureur and rue Frédéric-Mistral lead to rue de la République and the Musée Lapidaire, which contains archaeological finds from the Egyptian, Greek and Gallo-Roman periods. Tel: 04 90 85 75 38. Open: winter Wed–Sun 10am–1pm & 2–6pm; summer 10am–6pm. Admission charge.

Walk: Avignon

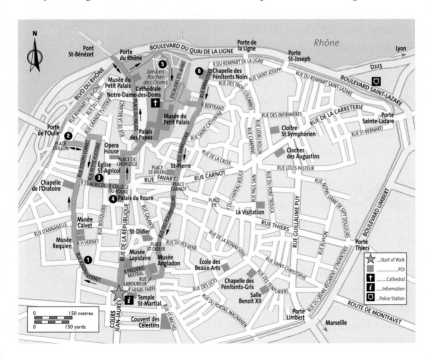

The popes

Provence played a notable part in the convoluted religious life of the Middle Ages when, in the 14th century, it became the seat of the papacy. This curious chapter in the history of Provence began in 1309 with the decision of Pope Clement V, who was French by birth, to set up court in a Dominican monastery in Avignon (he had never actually reached Rome since his election in 1305). He thus began what was unflatteringly described as 'the second Babylonian captivity of the Church', a period of preoccupation with power, legalism and money-raising.

The popes who followed his lead were a mixed bunch: Urban V was later beatified, but Benoit XII was regarded as uncharitable and avaricious, and Clement VI – of noble birth and with tastes to match – continued his love affair, ennobled his 'nephew' and built a sumptuous new palace reflecting his enthusiasm for the arts and high living. He also bought the city of Avignon (in return for absolution for the owner's sin of complicity in the murder of her first husband) for 80,000 florins, a sum only five times the cost of his inaugural banquet.

The Great Schism
In 1377 Pope Gregory XI, a Frenchman, was persuaded to move the Holy See back to Rome and try to restore order to the warring states. But the Italian Urban VI, who soon followed him in 1378, upset the

The Avignon papal palace is a symbol of worldly wealth

cardinals of France so much that they left Rome and elected a new French pope in his place, Clement VII, recognised by the King of France. Thus was born the Great Schism of 1378–1417, with one pope in Rome and another in France. Christendom was split in two, both geographically and politically, with the 'Clementines' drawn up against the 'Urbanists'. They excommunicated each other and issued bulls calling for crusades against each other. The death of one or other of the popes gave rise to fresh elections.

The two papacies were joined by a third in 1409, created by cardinals of the two parties hoping to find a compromise. Finally the crisis was resolved through a Church Council, at which a new pope was elected following the abdication or deposition of the other three.

Meanwhile, Avignon appears to have become exhausted by the controversy long before the Schism was resolved, for in 1403 the last of the Antipopes, Benoit XIII, was smuggled out of the Palais by a secret passage after a five-year siege by French troops, and the city settled into a more tranquil life. Even after the Schism, however, Avignon was governed by a succession of papal legates. It remained papal property until the French Revolution.

An ornate Madonna looks down from on high above the Notre-Dame-des-Doms, Avignon

Beaumes-de-Venise

This large village is known for its famous Muscat de Beaumes-de-Venise, a distinctive sweet amber-coloured wine. The village stands at the southern approach to the rugged Dentelles de Montmirail (*see p35*), about 10km (6 miles) north of Carpentras. Narrow terraced streets climb into the hillside from an attractive central square lined with cafés and shops.

One kilometre (²/₃ mile) to the west is the **Chapelle de Notre-Dame d'Aubune**, dating from the 9th and 10th centuries and topped by a Romanesque bell tower. Frankish and Saracen forces are said to have clashed here in the 8th century.

Wine-lovers will need no introduction to the villages around Beaumes – Vacqueyras, Gigondas, Sablet, Rasteau, Cairanne – for this area on the flattish eastern flank of the Rhône Valley produces the premier Côtes-du-Rhône Villages, a robust, peppery red wine of formidable strength.

Beaumes is 9km (5¹/₂ miles) north of Carpentras.

Bédoin

In winter, Bédoin is a sleepy village. In summer, it is transformed into a busy holiday centre. Do not try to drive through Bédoin on Monday morning, when the main street becomes a marketplace packed with stallholders and milling crowds.

Bédoin's popularity rests on its location. It stands at an altitude of over 300m (984ft), surrounded by beautiful

St-Siffrein's Cathedral at Carpentras

wooded hills on the southern slopes of Mont Ventoux. Campsites and holiday homes attract a cosmopolitan mix of visitors (the area is particularly popular with the Dutch). You can soak up the sunny atmosphere in one of the many cafés along Bédoin's long main street.

For the children, the village has an excellent municipal swimming pool. Historically, there is little evidence of Bédoin's ancient roots (it was founded in the 8th century), though there are vestiges of the medieval ramparts in the streets leading up to the hilltop church.

Bédoin is 15km (9 miles) northeast of Carpentras.

Carpentras

For visitors, interest in Carpentras lies within the historic heart of the town;

this is encircled by a ring of main arteries that follows the line of medieval fortifications (demolished in the 19th century). Compact central Carpentras is easily explored on foot. The towering Porte d'Orange, the main gateway into the old town from the north, is a lone, splendid medieval survivor. From this 14th-century gateway, the rue d'Orange and rue de l'Evêché lead into the pedestrianised town centre, dominated by the **Palais de Justice** (Law Courts) and the **Cathédrale St-Siffrein**. Guided tours of the Palais de Justice – formerly the episcopal palace, dating from the 17th century – are available in summer (enquire at the **Office de Tourisme**, *97 place du 25 Août 1944*). The cathedral, which is of limited interest, was started in 1404 and completed in the 17th century.

It is worth searching for the **Arc de Triomphe** hidden behind the Palais de Justice. This beautifully decorated Roman arch was probably built at about the same time as the more famous monument at Orange (*see p38*).

One of the Vaucluse's main markets is held in Carpentras each Friday morning. Look out for the stalls selling *berlingots*, the special caramel sweets for which the town is famous.

Musée Comtadin-Duplessis

Downstairs, the Musée Comtadin contains a wide-ranging collection of regional artefacts, including weapons, *santons* and bells worn by cattle and sheep. The Musée Duplessis, upstairs, displays the work of 18th-century Carpentras painter Joseph-Siffrein Duplessis and others.
234 boulevard Albert-Durand. Tel: 04 90 63 04 92. Open: Apr–Sept Wed–Mon 10am–noon & 2–6pm; Oct–Mar by appointment. Admission charge.

Synagogue

The oldest synagogue in France, this ancient building dates from the 14th century when Jews were banished from

Mont Ventoux provides the backdrop to the village of Bédoin

the Kingdom of France but were
granted refuge in Carpentras by Pope
Clement V. There is still a considerable
Jewish community living in the area.
Place Maurice Charretier.
Tel: 04 90 63 39 97. Open: Mon–Thur
10am–noon & 3–5pm, Fri till 4pm.
Closed: on Jewish holidays. Free
admission. Carpentras is 26km
(16 miles) northeast of Avignon.

Châteauneuf-du-Pape is synonymous with
fine wines

Cavaillon

Fruit and vegetable fields fill the
flattish, well-irrigated countryside
around Cavaillon. One product in
particular – the melon – is the mainstay
of the area's thriving market gardening
economy. Unsurprisingly, the town is
home to the second-largest wholesale
fruit and vegetable market in France.

For a panoramic view of the fertile
Cavaillon Plain, Mont Ventoux, the hills
of the Luberon and the Alpilles, follow
the path that climbs Colline St-Jacques
from the Roman Arch (re-erected here
in 1880) at place François-Tourel. On
the hill you will find the 12th-century
Chapelle St-Jacques, on the site of a
temple to Jupiter. Cavaillon's main
historic monument is the Cathédrale
St-Véran, though the town also contains
a richly decorated synagogue and small
museum. The latter reflect the town's
long-standing links with the Jewish
religion, for Cavaillon was one of four
Jewish centres – along with Avignon,
Carpentras and L'Isle-sur-la-Sorgue –
in the Comtat Venaissin, the land given
to the papacy by France in 1274.

Cathédrale St-Véran

This Romanesque cathedral dates from
the end of the 12th century. It was built
in the same elegant style as Avignon's
Cathédrale Notre-Dame-des-Doms.
Along place Voltaire.

Musée de l'Hôtel Dieu

Housed in the old hospital chapel, this
museum is devoted to local prehistory
and the Gallo-Roman period. Exhibits
include preserved Gaulish food.
At the intersection of Grand Rue and
cours Gambetta. Tel: 04 90 76 00 34.
Open: summer Wed–Sun 9.30am–
12.30pm & 2.30–6.30pm; Oct Wed–Sun
9am–noon & 2–5pm; winter by
appointment only. Admission charge.

Cavaillon is 24km (15 miles) southeast
of Avignon.

Châteauneuf-du-Pape

Châteauneuf-du-Pape was the summer
retreat of the 14th-century Avignon
popes. The remains of their château
overlook the Rhône Valley. Only one

tower and a stretch of walls survive. Most visitors are attracted by the area's highly refined wines (the popes are thought to have established the first vineyards here). There is a bemusing choice of *domaines* where you can taste this prized wine, which benefits from a favourable microclimate and a ground cover of large rounded pebbles that enables the grapes to reach a very high degree of maturity.

Nearby, on the opposite bank of the Rhône, is Roquemaure, another wine village with papal connnections, well-preserved old houses, a 13th-century church and a ruined castle.

Musée du Vin

The museum traces the history of wine in the area, with displays of medieval equipment. Includes a free wine tasting.

Maison Brotte, avenue Pierre de Luxembourg. Tel: 04 90 83 70 07. www.brotte.com. Open: winter 9am–noon & 2–6pm; summer 9am–1pm & 2–7pm. Free admission.

Châteauneuf-du-Pape is on the D17 between Avignon and Orange.

Dentelles de Montmirail

This striking line of hills flanks the eastern side of the Rhône Valley for 15km (9 miles) between Vaison-la-Romaine and Beaumes-de-Venise. Rising to 734m (2,446ft), they should be dwarfed by the 1,909m (6,263ft) summit of Mont Ventoux. Yet their strange, fiercely jagged profile – a complete contrast to Ventoux's smooth, uniform mass – imparts a presence almost matching that of their lofty neighbour.

The range takes its name from *dentelle*, meaning lace: the needle-sharp peaks and spikes of limestone rock, forced upright by the movement of the earth's crust and eroded by the wind, were thought to resemble the pins on a lacemaking board. Their white-grey summits, rising above slopes and hidden valleys covered in a thick coat of pine, oak and scrub, attract walkers, climbers, naturalists and painters – and, in autumn, seekers of wild mushrooms. While it is best to explore the Dentelles on foot, the D90 linking Beaumes-de-Venise with Malaucène is a spectacularly scenic road that loops through the mountains. The western slopes are dotted with famous Côtes-du-Rhône wine villages – Gigondas, Vacqueyras, Sablet and Séguret.

Fontaine-de-Vaucluse

Few visitors see Fontaine-de-Vaucluse at its most spectacular. The best time to visit this dramatic natural phenomenon is in the winter or spring, when the source of the River Sorgue, fed by rainwater from the Vaucluse Plateau above, rises from a deep hole at the base of a sheer cliff and tumbles over giant boulders down a narrow ravine.

But even in summer, when the source has retreated to a still, ominous pool beneath the cliff face leaving the river bed above bone dry, it is still an awesome sight. The Vaucluse Fountain is one of the most powerful resurgent springs in the world (it can pump water over its lip at the rate of 150,000 litres/ 33,000 gallons per second) and has been traced underground to a depth of over 300m (984ft) by a remote-controlled submarine.

Fontaine-de-Vaucluse's magnetic personality has attracted the inevitable clutch of gift shops and souvenir stalls, which line the riverside walk from the car parks to the spring. Summer crowds can be a problem, so plan your visit for early in the day – or lunchtime, if you can stand the heat. On your way to the fountain call in at the paper mill, where high-quality paper is still made the traditional way with the help of a giant waterwheel.

Ecomusée du Gouffre

This riverside visitor centre, in which an underground cave system has been re-created, explains the local spelaeology and the discoveries made at the fountain.
Chemin du Gouffre. Tel: 04 90 20 34 13. Open: Feb–mid-Nov 9.30am–12.30pm & 2–6.30pm. Last admission one hour before closing. Conducted tours in French. Admission charge.

Musée d'Histoire 1939–1945

A moving modern museum commemorating World War II and the resistance movement.
Chemin du Gouffre. Tel: 04 90 20 24 00. Open: Apr–May & Oct Wed–Mon
10am–noon & 2–6pm; Jun–Sept Wed–Mon 10am–6pm; Mar & Nov–Dec Sat–Sun 10am–noon & 2–6pm (Nov–Dec till 5pm). Admission charge.

Musée Pétrarque

Documents and books relating to the life of the 14th-century poet Petrarch can be seen in this small museum, together with a collection of modern art.
Rive gauche de la Sorgue. Tel: 04 90 20 37 20. Open: Apr–May & 1–15 Oct Wed–Mon 10am–noon & 2–6pm; Jun–Sept Wed–Mon 10am–12.30pm & 1.30–6pm; 15–31 Oct Wed–Mon 10am–noon & 2–5pm. Closed: Nov–Mar. Admission charge.

Fontaine-de-Vaucluse is on the D25, 24km (15 miles) southeast of Carpentras.

Gordes

Gordes is almost too good to be true. Overlooking the blue hills of the Luberon, this village of honey-coloured stone houses clings to a south-facing cliff on the edge of the Vaucluse Plateau. Renovated rustic dwellings, villas and discreet hotels, each one complete with the obligatory swimming pool, help create an idyllic vision of Provençal life.

The village is much favoured by the French elite – actors, politicians, media personalities and artists. This status is confirmed by the breathtaking prices displayed by local *immobiliers* (estate agents).

Despite its chic nature, Gordes's historic fabric shines through. From the medieval château in the centre of the village, steep cobbled alleyways, lined with an incongruous mixture of fashionable boutiques, immaculate holiday homes and yet-to-be-restored houses, weave a confusing path down the precipitous hillside.

Abbaye de Sénanque

The medieval abbey, one of three founded by the Cistercians in Provence, is still in use and also open to the public for guided tours in French, although (depending on the time of day) you can also walk around by yourself. The abbey's lavender fields are an iconic image of Provence. Note that suitable dress is required.
About 4km (2 1/2 miles) north of Gordes on the D177. Tel: 04 90 72 05 72. www. senanque.fr. Telephone for opening hours. Closed: Sun morning. Admission charge.

Château de Gordes

This solid-looking castle, flanked by round corner towers, dates from 1031 and was rebuilt in 1525. The castle's Renaissance interior houses the Musée Pol Mara, which displays the work of Belgian artist Pol Mara (1920–98).
Village centre. Tel: 04 90 72 02 75. Open: daily 10am–noon & 2–6pm. Admission charge.

Village des Bories

Although the *bories* (dry-stone huts) in this amazing village and museum of

rural life are prehistoric in appearance, they were in fact built between 200 and 500 years ago. The curving, cone-like roofs display craftsmanship of the highest order.
Signposted about 3km (2 miles) southwest of Gordes off the D2. Tel: 04 90 72 03 48. Open: daily 9am–sunset. Admission charge.

Gordes is off the D2, 20km (12 miles) west of Apt.

L'Isle-sur-la-Sorgue

Antique hunters and lovers of bric-brac spend hours poring through the myriad furniture and decorative bargains in this delightful canal-side town, once noted for its fishing and fabrics industry. Some of its old water wheels can still be seen. The weekend market, renowned throughout the country, adds a further dimension to its genteel air.
About 18km (11 miles) south of Carpentras.

Fontaine-de-Vaucluse, where the River Sorgue emerges from its source

Orange

Visitors arrive with preconceptions of a Roman town *par excellence* and are never disappointed with Orange's awesome Théâtre Antique (amphitheatre) and the wonderfully decorative Arc de Triomphe Roman archway. But take these ancient monuments away, and you are left with a fairly ordinary Provençal town blessed with a traffic system that defies any form of logic.

The medieval heart of Orange, just north of the Théâtre Antique, though it lacks the personality of other old town centres in this part of the world, is a pleasant place, with open, fountained squares, cafés and shops. To the south, on a high bluff above the Théâtre Antique, is the Parc de la Colline St-Eutrope, with a beautiful viewpoint overlooking the town, the rich vineyards of the Rhône Plain, and the Marcoule nuclear power station. This outcrop was the site of a castle (now in ruins) of the princes of Orange-Nassau, destroyed in 1663.

Despite the name, it was in another, much earlier era that Orange's true identity was established. The Romans founded a colony here in 35 BC, leaving the town with a unique legacy. The amphitheatre that goes back to that era is today said to be the best-preserved Roman theatre in the world. We have Maurice, son of William the Silent, to thank for its survival. He incorporated the theatre's massive wall into the town's fortification, to the benefit of both. Orange's Arc de Triomphe is another remarkable survivor.

Arc de Triomphe

Built in about 20 BC, this triple-arched monument stands 22m (72ft) high and is decorated with scenes recalling the Roman conquest of Gaul.
On the northern approach to the town – follow avenue de l'Arc de Triomphe from the centre.

Cathédrale Notre-Dame-de-Nazareth

This Romanesque cathedral, originally founded in 529, suffered great damage during the 16th-century Wars of Religion. Look out for the ancient carvings on the south porch.
Along rue Notre-Dame off rue Victor-Hugo.

Musée Municipale

Exhibits from Orange's Roman and medieval past include a fascinating Roman land survey and artefacts from the ruined castle.
Rue Madeleine-Roch. Tel: 04 90 51 17 60. Open: Jan, Feb, Nov & Dec daily 9am–4.30pm; Mar & Oct daily 9.30am–5.30pm; Apr–Sept daily 9am–7pm. Admission charge.

Théâtre Antique
(Roman Amphitheatre)

This theatre, built during the reign of Augustus, is an awesome sight. Looking down from the steep-sided semicircle of terraced seats to the stage, you gaze at virtually the same backdrop that must

THE HOUSE OF ORANGE

In 1572 William the Silent, Prince of Orange and Nassau, laid the foundation for the House of Orange when he was elected William I, Stadholder of the Low Countries – the Netherlands. The title passed on to his sons, who allied the House of Orange through marriage to the other powerful Protestant families of Europe: the Hohenzollerns in Prussia and the Stuarts in England.

have caught the imagination of audiences 2,000 years ago. The stage wall still stands 36m (118ft) high, decorated with columns, niches, frescoes and a large, suitably imperious statue of Augustus. The theatre's superb acoustics continue to be put to good use. Audiences of 10,000 gather here during Orange's famous summer festival of opera and choral music. Beside the amphitheatre are the ruins of a huge gymnasium, baths and temple complex, with three 180m (591ft) running tracks and a raised platform for gladiatorial combat.
Place des Frères-Mounet.
Open: as for Musée Municipale.
Admission charge.

Orange is on the N7, about 21km (13 miles) north of Avignon.

Roussillon

Roussillon's architecture is a mirror image of its surroundings. The deep reds, yellows, rusty oranges and other burnished tones of its houses reflect the different shades of ochre rock found in its surrounding hills. This area's soft

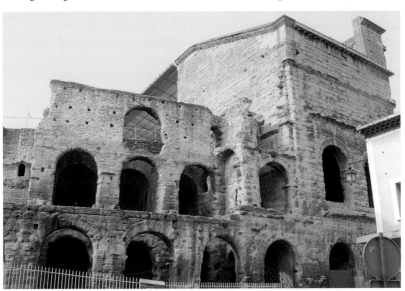

Orange's great Roman theatre is still in use, notably for the town's summer music festival

rocks have been quarried and mined since prehistoric times for their natural dye. Mining peaked in the late 1920s, when 40,000 tons of ochre were exported from the region. By the early 1950s the industry was in terminal decline, and the last ochre was mined in Roussillon in 1958.

The village's vibrantly coloured dwellings, arranged haphazardly in narrow, winding streets around a pronounced hill, have given it a new lease of life: Roussillon is now a place that everyone wants to see, paint and photograph. Park your car at the approach and follow rue de l'Arcade to a superb viewpoint overlooking the Vaucluse Plateau, Mont Ventoux, the Coulon Valley and the Luberon Mountains. From vantage points south and southeast of the village, you can gaze over the **Aiguilles du Val des Fées** (Needles of Fairies' Valley) and the **Chaussée des Géants** (Giants' Causeway), strangely weathered areas of rust-red rocks and cliffs.

Roussillon is off the N100, about 10km (6 miles) northwest of Apt.

The rock of the surrounding country gives Roussillon's buildings their red-gold shades

Rustrel Colorado

The explosive intensity of colours in the abandoned, canyon-like ochre quarries of Rustrel Colorado has to be seen to be believed. Ranging from blood-red to bright yellow, exposed cliff faces and weathered pinnacles consisting entirely of crumbly, sandy rock fill the valley south of the village of Rustrel. A number of trails lead into this otherworldly place. The easiest access is from the car parks beside the River Doua southwest and southeast of Rustrel, starting points for well-defined paths into the Colorado.

Rustrel Colorado is off the D22, about 8km (5 miles) northeast of Apt.

Sault

Standing at an exhilarating 765m (2,510ft), Sault displays yet another of Provence's many faces. On the high, open Vaucluse Plateau with sweeping vistas westwards to Mont Ventoux, Sault and its surroundings have an almost Alpine air. The fields beneath this unpretentious, easy-going town are a patchwork of purple in high summer, when the lavender is in full bloom. The entire town is swamped in its sweet fragrance during the annual Lavender Festival, held in mid-August. Lavender cultivation and distillation is an important part of the local economy. So too is the manufacture of nougat. The Boyer family of Sault claim that their nougat, not the better-known Montélimar variety, is the real thing. *Sault is on the eastern approach to Mont Ventoux, 41km (25 miles) east of Carpentras.*

Séguret

Séguret is one of those impossibly picturesque villages that only the French seem capable of creating. Mellow, wheat-coloured houses with terracotta tiled roofs cling to a steep slope above the vineyards of the northern Vaucluse. So well is Séguret integrated into its surroundings that when the sun strikes directly on to its stonework it almost disappears, chameleon-like, into the rocky background of the Dentelles de Montmirail (*see p35*).

The village's ridiculously narrow streets were not made for cars. From the car park at the western approach, walk up into the village through the ancient gateway to the 15th-century Mascarons Fountain. Over the last couple of decades, Séguret has been 'discovered' by artists and visitors, yet it has managed to avoid the commercial excesses of other hill villages. A medieval atmosphere still pervades its cobbled alleyways, vaulted passageways, nooks and crannies. Each Christmas the 12th-century church is decorated with *santons*, intricately detailed figurines depicting the Nativity (*see p125*). *Santons* and Séguret go together: there are a number of makers in the village, one of whom has an enchanting display from around the world. *Séguret is off the D977, 10km (6 miles) southwest of Vaison-la-Romaine.*

Vaison-la-Romaine

Try to visit Vaison on a Tuesday morning, when the town holds one of the biggest street markets in Provence. Place de Montfort – Vaison's attractive central square – and almost all of the streets leading to it are filled with greengrocers, fishmongers, cheesemakers, antique dealers, painters, craftspeople, florists, musicians, entertainers and sellers of household goods. This is not a show put on for the tourists: markets are a way of life in Provence.

For the rest of the week, Vaison is a calm and surprisingly cosmopolitan small Provençal town. It is popular with visitors for its location, in seductive, rolling countryside between the Rhône Valley and Mont Ventoux, and its underrated, magnificent Roman remains.

The Romans made a comfortable home for themselves in Vaison. You can still wander round the streets of their excavated town, or watch a summer concert in the 7,000-seat amphitheatre.

(*Cont. on p44*)

Vaucluse

Lavender and flowers

The flowers of Provence are among its greatest treasures. Their heady mix of colours and scents makes a vivid impression on the senses, not only catching the eye of the casual observer but providing inspiration for the artist and a fertile field of study for the naturalist.

Nature is at its most prodigal in April and May, when sheets of spring flowers cloak the fields and hills. High summer brings out the gaudy brilliance of the sunflower, which Van Gogh captured so well on canvas. But it is typical of the sheer unexpectedness of Provence that the region should also harbour the delicate beauty of the arctic flora that clings to the upper slopes of Mont Ventoux, despite the Mediterranean influences at the foot of the mountain.

No self-respecting resort is without that symbol of the Côte d'Azur, the palm tree. Other subtropical and exotic species, in gardens all along the Riviera, also take root in this sunny, sheltered habitat.

The scent of lavender

It is, perhaps, the lavender that imprints itself most vividly upon the memory of the visitor. In this sun-soaked region it grows abundantly, staining the fields a delicate purple and scenting the air in July and August. This pungent scent is captured second-hand in the

For many, lavender is synonymous with the region

Provence in bloom

perfumes of Provence. Golden mimosa, jonquils, roses, thyme, violets and yellow broom are also gathered – some would say plundered – to provide the raw material for the perfumer's art. The flower markets also do a brisk trade in the towns and villages of Provence, and mimosa is cultivated for export in winter.

Hidden away

The *maquis* – not a single plant, but a community of dense Mediterranean brush – half-conceals an amazing variety of floral life, including rosemary and juniper, tree heathers and broom. Orchids are plentiful in some districts. The herbs of Provence have not only played a central role in regional cuisine, but have traditionally provided remedies for many an ill.

Provence has a lot to offer the naturalist

The Roman single-arched bridge survived the devastating floods in Vaison in the autumn of 1992, when unrelenting storms, held in place by Mont Ventoux, transformed the River Ouvèze into a tidal wave, swamping the lower town. Vaison's Haute-Ville (Upper Town) was untouched by the floodwater.

The rock above the Ouvèze is crowned by an abandoned castle, a wonderful viewpoint accessible by climbing through the narrow, cobbled streets of Old Vaison, a charming and now fashionable place with fountains and fine Renaissance houses.

Ancienne Cathédrale Notre-Dame-de-Nazareth

Built on the foundations of a large Roman monument, this fine cathedral in Provençal Romanesque style dates from the 12th and 13th centuries. Its beautiful cloisters, attached to the northern wall, are particularly noteworthy.

Avenue Louis-Blanc. Cloisters open: 9 Feb–8 Mar 3–7pm; Apr–Jun 3–6pm; Jul–Sept 10am–12.30pm & 2–6.30pm; Oct 10am–noon & 2–5pm. Admission charge.

Ruines Romaines

Such is the extent of these ruins that they are split into two sections – Quartier de Puymin and Quartier de la Villasse – divided by the avenue du Général de Gaulle, which leads into the town centre. All in all, they give us a rare insight into everyday life in the 1st century AD.

Quartier de Puymin, built around a small hill, contains the Théâtre Antique (amphitheatre), the Portique

The medieval town of Vaison-la-Romaine towers over the remains of a Roman city

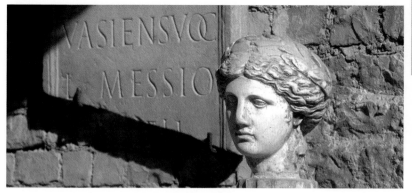

Vaison-la-Romaine shelters the most complete Roman town to be discovered in France

de Pompée (Pompey's Portico), a beautiful colonnaded area that probably served as a public garden, and the remains of residences both modest and grand. The museum, full of finds excavated in Vaison, is also located here.

Quartier de la Villasse contains an amazing paved main street, complete with drains and the remains of shops, together with baths, large houses and colonnades. You can get a two-day pass allowing you to visit all Vaison's main sights.

Accessible off avenue du Général de Gaulle. Tel: 04 90 36 50 00 (town hall). Open: Mar–May daily 10am–12.30pm & 2–6pm; Jun–Sept daily 9.30am–6.30pm; Oct–Feb daily 10am–noon & 2–5pm. Guided visits in English from Easter to end Oct by appointment (tel: 04 90 36 50 48). Admission charge.

Vaison-la-Romaine is 29km (18 miles) north of Carpentras.

Vénasque

Vénasque sits astride a steep rock overlooking the Gorges de la Nesque. Its natural defensive position was augmented in medieval times by towers and walls, giving the pretty village, once the bishopric of the Comtat Venaissin, to which it gave its name, an even more self-contained air. Its famous baptistery, probably dating from the 6th century, is one of France's oldest religious buildings. The 13th-century **Église de Notre-Dame** beside the baptistery is also of interest.

From Vénasque, you can follow a twisting road to another fascinating religious site, the Abbaye de Sénanque (*see p37*). Nearby is **Pernes-les-Fontaines**, a working market town that preserves a wonderful array of old monuments, including medieval walls, a tower, gateways, chapels, Renaissance streets and, of course, fountains – 36 in all!

Vénasque is 11km (7 miles) southeast of Carpentras on the D4.

Tour: Mont Ventoux

Wherever you travel in the Vaucluse, you take Mont Ventoux (the 'Windy Mountain') with you. This towering landmark, 1,909m (6,263ft) high, is visible from all corners.

Allow at least half a day for the tour.

From Vaison-la-Romaine (see pp41–5) take the D938 to Malaucène.

1 Malaucène

Malaucène's pleasant main street is lined with plane trees, cafés and restaurants. The old town, a maze of alleyways, tall houses and fountains, preserves an authentic Provençal atmosphere. Malaucène's proximity to Mont Ventoux makes it a lively tourist centre in summer and a major base for hiking, riding and cycling expeditions.

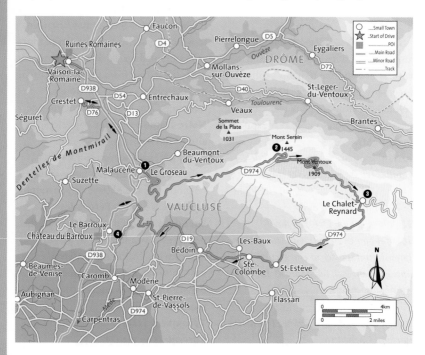

A short distance from the town, on the road up to Mont Ventoux, is Le Groseau, a spring that emerges from a rocky fissure to form a clear pool surrounded by trees and picnic tables.

The D974 climbs through beautiful wooded countryside on the north-facing slopes of Ventoux. Up until the ski station of Mont Serein, the road is wide, with sweeping, well-engineered bends.

2 Mont Serein

At 1,445m (4,740ft), Mont Serein is a modest ski resort, busy at weekends in winter with skiers from Avignon (the mountain is usually snowcapped above 1,400m (4,595ft) from December to March).

The final climb to the summit of Mont Ventoux from Mont Serein is the most spectacular part of the ascent. The road becomes narrower, the bends more severe – and the drops more vertiginous! For the final 300m (984ft) or so, the forests of pine, oak, cedar, beech and larch give way to a bare expanse of broken rock, a strange, barren environment. Stranger still are the monumental buildings and sinister-looking installations on the summit; these are used for telecommunications, air-force radar and meteorological purposes. The panorama from the top is one of the best in Europe. On a clear day, looking down into the valley of the Toulourenc or across to the jagged peaks of the Alps gives a fleeting impression of flight.

From the summit, the D974 descends to Le Chalet-Reynard, Ventoux's smaller, southern ski station.

3 Le Chalet-Reynard

Before Le Chalet-Reynard, you will see a small roadside monument in homage to British cyclist Tommy Simpson, who suffered heart failure here on 13 July 1967 while competing in the Tour de France. It was one of the hottest days ever recorded in the race.

Continue on the D974 to Bédoin (see p32) and the scenic D19, which brings you to the D938. Here, you can take a short detour south to Le Barroux.

4 Le Barroux

The restored **Château du Barroux** (*tel: 04 90 62 35 21*), dating from the 12th century and remodelled in the 16th, stands on a rocky outcrop overlooking the village.

On the way back to Vaison, take another short detour along the D76 for Crestet, a picturesque village perched high above the valley of the Ouvèze. Hidden in the slopes beyond the village is a fascinating collection of woodland sculptures.

The majestic Mont Ventoux

Bouches-du-Rhône

Bordered by the Durance to the north and the Rhône to the west, the Bouches-du-Rhône is one of the oldest inhabited regions of Provence, with some of the best monuments from Roman and medieval times. The mighty Rhône meets the Mediterranean among the reedy flatlands of the Camargue, a truly distinctive part of Provence with an identity all of its own.

Abbaye-de-Montmajour

This imposing ruin, which occupies a slight rise in the Rhône delta's flatlands northeast of Arles, is easily spotted. It was founded in the 10th century by the Benedictines, an industrious group of monks who set about draining and reclaiming the marshlands of this low-lying area. In 1791, after a troubled few centuries, the abbey was sold and its assets stripped. Luckily, the people of Arles adopted the building in the 19th century, restoring it little by little. Much remains from the abbey's early period: a 12th-century church with a fine vaulted crypt, cloisters (again 12th-century, but rebuilt in later times), monastic buildings, a tall, castellated abbey tower constructed to defend the abbey in 1369 and, next door to the tower, a tiny chapel carved out of the hillside.

On the D17 between Arles and Fontvieille. Tel: 04 90 54 64 17. Open: Apr–Jun daily 9.30am–6pm; Jul–Sept daily 10am–6.30pm; Oct–Mar Tue–Sun 10am–5pm (closed: Mon). Admission charge.

Abbaye de Silvacane

This 12th-century abbey is one of the Cistercians' 'three Provençal sisters' – the others being Sénanque (*see p37*) and Thoronet (*see p134*). From its setting above the River Durance, it looks across to the foothills of the Luberon.

The abbey's plain, uncluttered lines reflect the Cistercians' firm belief in simplicity. Its church, built into a steep slope, is devoid of any decoration. The daily routine of the monks is brought to life in some of the abbey's other buildings, which include a library, chapterhouse, warming house, dormitory and large refectory complete with pulpit. Following a period of decline, it became the village church for **La Roque-d'Anthéron** in the early 16th century, but was later abandoned.

On the D561, northeast of Salon-de-Provence. Tel: 04 42 50 41 69. Open: Jun–Sept daily 10am–6pm; Oct–May Wed–Sun 10am–1pm & 2–5pm. Admission charge.

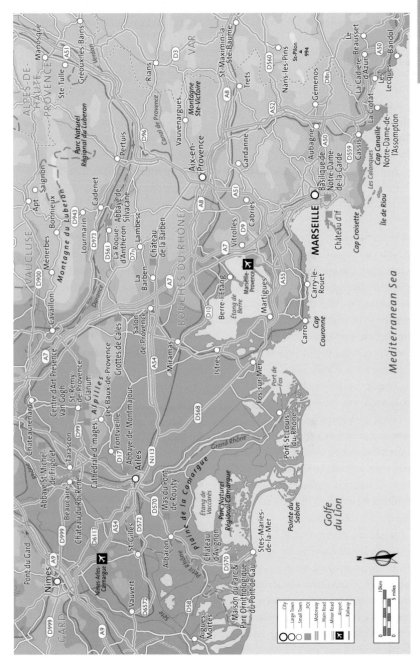

ALPES-DE-HAUTE-PROVENCE

VAR

Manosque
Ste-Tulle
Gréoux-les-Bains
A51
Verdon
Rians
D3
St-Maximin-la-Ste-Baume
St-Pilon
994
Nans-les-Pins
D560
La Cadière d'Azur
Île
Beausset
A50
Bandol
Col de Provence
Trets
Gémenos
D8n
Les Lecques
Parc Naturel Régional du Luberon
Montagne Ste-Victoire
A8
La Ciotat
Apt
Saignon
Pertuis
Aubagne
A50
D559
Cassis
Cap Canaille
Notre-Dame-de-l'Assomption
Bonnieux
Menerbes
Cadenet
Aix-en-Provence
Gardanne
Basilique-de-Notre-Dame-de-la-Garde
Les Calanques
D900
Abbaye de Silvacane
D943
A8
A51
Cabriès
Île de Riou
VAUCLUSE
Cavaillon
Lourmarin
La Roque d'Anthéron
D973
D561
Château de la Barben
Vitrolles
D9
MARSEILLE
Château d'If
Cap Croisette
Montagne du Luberon
D7n
Lambesc
A7
A55
Mediterranean Sea
La Barben
Salon-de-Provence
Marseille-Provence
Carry-le-Rouet
Durance
BOUCHES-DU-RHÔNE
A7
Berre-l'Étang
Étang de Berre
Martigues
Cap Couronne
Châteaurenard
Centre d'Art Présence Van Gogh
St-Rémy-de-Provence
Miramas
A54
D10
Carro
Tarascon
D99
Glanum
Alpilles
Les Baux-de-Provence
Grottes de Calès
Istres
Fos-sur-Mer
Port de Fos
Abbaye St-Michel-de-Frigolet
Château du Roi René
Cathédrale d'images
Fontvieille
Abbaye-de-Montmajour
D17
D568
Port-St-Louis-du-Rhône
Beaucaire
N113
Grand Rhône
D999
Arles
Pont du Gard
A9
Château d'Avignon
Mas du Pont de Rousty
Étang de Vaccarès
Parc Naturel Régional Camargue
Golfe du Lion
GARD
D611B
St-Gilles
D570
D572
Albaron
Plaine de la Camargue
Pointe du Sablon
A54
Nîmes
Nîmes-Arles-Camargue
Vauvert
Petit Rhône
D58
Maison du Parc & Parc Ornithologique du Pont-de-Gau
Stes-Maries-de-la-Mer
D999
Aigues-Mortes
D572
Sète
N

0 10km
0 5 miles

City
Large Town
Small Town
POI
Motorway
Main Road
Minor Road
Railway
Airport

Aix-en-Provence

Take a stroll along cours Mirabeau on a warm summer's day and you could be forgiven for thinking that you are in Paris. The wide street, lined with pavement cafés, plane trees, mossy fountains and handsome 17th- and 18th-century buildings, must surely have been built for promenading.

Aix (founded as Aquae Sextiae by the Romans), more than any other city in Provence, has an air of completeness. This may have something to do with its splendid situation poised between country and coast, with none of the rusticity of the former or the crass commercialism of the latter. It may also be due to a well-balanced blend of age groups – the youth of Aix's large student influx balanced against an affluent, worldly resident population. Whatever the reasons, it is a winning formula.

The city authorities have further enhanced Aix's intrinsic appeal by treating the historic centre with loving care and attention, and arts events are an important feature of local life. Wherever you look, you will be reminded of Aix's historic status as capital of Provence, a position it held from the 12th century to the French Revolution.

Start your exploration at La Rotonde, a monumental roundabout with a fabulous fountained centrepiece. From here, walk along cours Mirabeau, which more or less acts as the southern boundary to Aix's historic heart (though the Mazarin Quarter, built between 1645 and 1651 by Archbishop Michel Mazarin, lies further south again).

Take any of the streets north and you are soon in the Aix of old. Place d'Albertas, for example, has a lovely cobbled courtyard and fountain flanked by 18th-century houses with wrought-iron balconies. Place Richelme, the site of a daily vegetable market, is another pleasant open space, next door to the even more spacious place de l'Hôtel de Ville. There are, perhaps, too many immaculate open spaces to appreciate them all in one visit. Architecture buffs will be similarly satiated with an overload of richly decorated 16th- to 18th-century mansions – the Hôtel de Ville, for instance, its classical features carved into warm stone.

Atelier Cézanne (Cézanne's Studio)

Impressionist painter Paul Cézanne (1839–1906) was inspired by the light,

Cézanne's studio remains unchanged

colour and surroundings of his birthplace, Aix. His studio has been left as it was at his death.
9 avenue Paul-Cézanne. Tel: 04 42 21 06 53. www.atelier-cezanne.com. Open: Apr–Jun & Sept daily 10am–noon & 2–6pm; Jul & Aug daily 10am–6pm; Oct–Mar daily 10am–noon & 2–5pm. Admission charge.

Cathédrale St-Sauveur

Spanning the 5th to 16th centuries, this fascinating religious site – a mixture of ornate and restrained influences – is a lesson in ecclesiastical architecture. Filled with medieval art treasures, it also boasts delightful Romanesque cloisters displaying spiralling, flowing stone-carving of the highest order.
At the north end of rue Gaston-de-Saporta.

Fondation Vasarely

The exciting work of 20th-century artist Victor Vasarely is difficult to categorise. A visit to his arts and architecture centre is a stimulating experience.
Avenue Marcel-Pagnol, Jas-de-Bouffan. Tel: 04 42 20 01 09. www.fondationvasarely.fr. Open: Tue–Sat 10am–1pm & 2–6pm. Admission charge.

Jas de Bouffan

This fine house, once owned by Cézanne's father, is where the artist painted from 1860 to 1895. Now owned by the city, it has been open to the public since 2006.

Route de Galice. Guided tours only. Check times and buy tickets from the tourist office, 2 place du Général de Gaulle. Tel: 04 42 16 10 91.

Musée Estienne de St-Jean

The museum recalls Aix's aristocratic past and popular traditions.
17 rue Gaston-de-Saporta. Tel: 04 42 21 43 55. Open: Tue–Sun 10am–noon & 2.30–5pm (2–6pm in summer). Admission charge.

Musée Granet

Aix's modernised fine art museum houses mostly French paintings from the 16th century onwards, as well as Italian and Dutch works. It is home to eight Cézannes, and has a section devoted to Celto-Ligurian archaeological exhibits.
Place St-Jean-de-Malte. Tel: 04 42 52 88 32. www.museegranet-aixenprovence.fr. Open: Jun–Sept Tue–Sun 11am–7pm; Oct–May noon–6pm. Last admission one hour before closing. Admission charge.

Musée des Tapisseries (Tapestry Museum)

Famous tapestries and panels displayed in a former archbishops' palace.
28 place des Martyrs-de-la-Résistance. Tel: 04 42 23 09 91. Open: Wed–Mon 10am–12.30pm & 1.30–4.45pm. Admission charge.

Aix-en-Provence is located about 30km (19 miles) north of Marseille off the A8.

Arles

Visitors attracted to Arles on the strength of the town's Roman past and the canvases of Vincent Van Gogh, its most celebrated resident, might expect to find a surfeit of upmarket shops and expensive cafés. But the town wears its fame lightly. Despite streets packed with monuments and museums, Arles maintains an honest, everyday quality.

The Romans established a major base here and the town continued to prosper in medieval times as an important trading and religious centre, and base for the Counts of Provence. Vincent Van Gogh arrived in Arles in 1888 and sang its praises to his colleague Paul Gauguin.

The Alyscamps

Wooded avenues of ancient tombs and mausoleums line this early Christian necropolis southeast of the town centre. *Avenue des Alyscamps. Tel: 04 90 49 38 20. Open: Nov–Feb daily 10–noon & 2–5pm; Mar & Apr daily 9am–noon & 2–6pm; May–Sept daily 9am–7pm; Oct daily 9am–noon & 2–6pm. Admission charge.*

Arènes (Roman Amphitheatre)

This enormous oval, dating from the end of the 1st century, became a fortress in medieval times. It was later transformed into a small township of 200 houses. Nineteenth-century restoration has largely returned it to its former glory, though its third floor has disappeared. The arena is the setting for several traditional events, particularly in summer.
Rond-Point des Arènes. Tel: 04 90 49 38 20. Open: May–Sept daily 9am–7pm; Mar, Apr & Oct daily 9am–6pm; Nov–Feb daily 10am–5pm. Admission charge.

Fondation Vincent Van Gogh

Works by leading contemporary artists, sculptors and photographers pay

The Arènes is a superbly preserved Roman amphitheatre

homage here to the great painter.
Palais de Luppé, 26 Rond-Point des Arènes. Tel: 04 90 49 94 04. www.fondationvangogh-arles.org. Open: Apr–Jun daily 10am–6pm; Jul–Sept daily 10am–7pm; Oct–Mar Tue–Sun daily 11am–5pm. Admission charge.

Musée d'Arles Antique

In a striking contemporary building, ancient Arles comes to life through a superb collection of sarcophagi, sculpture and architectural details. Incorporating exhibits from the former Museum of Christian Art, this is a spacious and well-displayed museum.
Presqu'ille du Cirque Romain. Tel: 04 90 18 88 88. Open: Apr–mid-Sept daily 9am–7pm; mid-Sept–Mar Wed–Mon 10am–6pm. Admission charge.

Musée Réattu

Founded by the painter Réattu (1760–1833), the museum is famous for its Picassos and its fine photography collection.
10 rue du Grande Prieuré. Tel: 04 90 49 37 58. Open: Nov–Feb Tues–Sun 1–5pm; Mar, Apr & Oct Tues–Sun 10am–noon & 2–5pm; May & Jun Tues–Sun 10am–noon & 2–6.30pm; Jul–Sept Tues–Sun 10am–7pm. Admission charge.

Museon Arlaten

Poet Frédéric Mistral established this museum reflecting traditional Provençal life, crafts and customs at the turn of the 20th century.

25 rue de la République. Tel: 04 90 93 58 11. Open: Jun–Aug daily (closed Mon in Jun) 9.30am–1pm & 2–6.30pm; Apr, May & Sept Tue–Sun 9.30am–12.30pm & 2–6pm. Admission charge.

Primatiale St-Trophime

The cathedral's main doorway is probably the most accomplished example of 12th-century Provençal stone-carving in existence. The elaborate decorations are, literally, of biblical proportions.
Place de la République. Tel: 04 90 49 38 20. Cathedral open: daily 10am–noon & 2–6pm. Free admission.
Cloisters open: May–Sept daily 9am–7pm; Mar, Apr & Oct daily 9am–6pm; Nov–Feb daily 10am–5pm. Admission charge.

Théâtre Antique (Roman Theatre)

There is not much antiquity left at this open-air theatre, but it is a pleasant venue for summer performances.
Rue de la Calade (close to the Arènes). Tel: 04 90 49 36 74. Open: Nov–Feb daily 10am–noon & 1–5pm; Mar, Apr & Oct daily 9am–noon & 2–6pm; May–Sept daily 9am–7pm. Admission charge.

Thermes de Constantin (Baths of Constantine)

These 4th-century baths are all that remain of a Roman palace.
Rue Dominique-Maïsto. Tel: 04 90 49 36 74. Open: Nov–Feb daily 10am–11.30am & 2–4.30pm; Mar, Apr & Oct daily 9–11.30am & 2–5.30pm; May–Sept daily 9am–noon & 2–6pm. Admission charge.

Walk: Arles

Arles looks after its walkers well. The places of interest, mostly within a relatively small area, are bounded by the mighty Rhône to the north, the Arènes (Roman amphitheatre) to the east, and the Espace Van Gogh to the west. To make it even easier, all the main sites are well signposted.

Allow half a day for the walk: extra time for museum visits.

Begin the walk at the Office de Tourisme on boulevard des Lices. Walk along rue Jean-Jaurès to place de la République.

1 Place de la République

Place de la République, Arles' central square, is a large, open space, uncluttered by street-café parasols. The square's impressive dimensions, and the stature of the buildings that surround it, are immediately apparent. Overlooking the fountain and 15m (50ft) high Roman obelisk are the Clock Tower and Hôtel de Ville (Town Hall), its classical 17th-century façade reminiscent of Versailles. To one side is the Ancienne Église Ste-Anne. But the square's chief glory is the wonderfully decorative main doorway of the Primatiale St-Trophime.

From the Place, take rue de la Calade, which leads to the Théâtre Antique (Roman theatre), Arènes (Roman amphitheatre) and Fondation Vincent Van Gogh.

2 Arènes

The Arènes may not seem quite as high as you anticipated: its third storey has disappeared and the pavement around the monument is elevated for much of the way. Halfway around the Arènes, at the place de la Major, visit the **Collégiale Notre-Dame-de-la-Major**, a Romanesque collegiate church built close to surviving sections of the city ramparts. *Opposite the main steps to the Arènes, follow rue du l'Amphithéâtre (or the prettier, adjacent rue Voltaire, in which case take two left turns to get back to rue du 4 Septembre), turning left into rue du 4 Septembre. Turn right by the Église St-Julien along rue St-Julien to the riverbank of the Rhône (note the remains of the Roman bridge to the north). A ramped pathway runs along the riverside to the Musée Réattu – the entrance is along rue du Grande Prieuré.*

3 Thermes de Constantin

Only a short distance from the Musée Réattu are the Thermes de Constantin

(Baths of Constantine), accessible along rue Dominique-Maïsto.

Continue along this street for rue de l'Hôtel-de-Ville, turning right into rue des Arènes, which brings you to place du Forum.

4 Place du Forum

This small, charming square, lined with cafés and restaurants, is Arles' social hub. On a summer's night, it is easy to see where Van Gogh's inspiration for *Café Evening* came from. A statue of Provençal poet and Nobel Prize-winner Frédéric Mistral stands close to the Hôtel Nord-Pinus, whose façade contains two columns

from a 2nd-century Roman temple. *Leave place du Forum by rue du Palais, turning right along rue Balze. Then turn left into rue Frédéric-Mistral, then left again into rue de la République – one of Arles' main shopping streets – for the Museon Arlaten. Close to the museum, along rue du Président-Wilson, is the Espace Van Gogh.*

5 Espace Van Gogh

Espace Van Gogh, inaugurated in 1989, is the old Hôtel-Dieu hospital in which the artist spent time after cutting off his ear lobe. It is now a cultural centre with a garden, small workshops and souvenir shops (*open: Tue, Wed, Fri & Sat*).

Arles

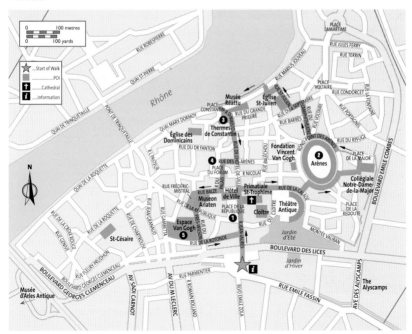

Van Gogh

The name of the Dutch painter Vincent Van Gogh (1853–90) is ineradicably linked with Provence. The region shimmers with heightened colour and vibrancy in the loud, swirling canvases he painted here towards the end of his troubled life.

Van Gogh, the son of a pastor, trained for the ministry himself, but he was reproached for 'excessive zeal' by his superiors when he gave many of his possessions to the poor. He decided to become an artist and was kept alive principally by a regular allowance from his younger brother Théo.

The artist himself – from a poster in Arles

The lure of the south

Self-taught as an artist, he was influenced by the new French Impressionist movement led by Monet, Renoir and Degas and lived in the Montmartre area of Paris for two years. He then moved to the South of France, bewitched by its dazzling light and colours, and rented a house in Arles in 1888. Inspired by the idea of an artists' colony, he persuaded his friend Paul Gauguin to join him, but the two soon fell out. After a fierce row, Van Gogh cut off the lobe of his right ear and sent it to a prostitute in an envelope.

Blossoming creativity

Despite – or perhaps because of – his emotional state, his 14 months in Arles were the most productive of his life. During this short period, he produced hundreds of paintings and drawings. Van Gogh was never popular in the town, where he was

The artist's painting of a Provence farmhouse

jeered at as a 'madman', and none of his works can be found in the local art museums. The sunflowers and cypresses he depicted so vividly still grow in abundance, however, and his personal experience of Provence is captured in such works as the portrait of his friend Roulin the postman, his painting of his bedroom in Arles, and the swirling colours of his magical *Starry Night* series.

In 1889, fear of madness prompted him to commit himself voluntarily to an asylum in St-Rémy-de-Provence, where he was allowed to paint in the gardens. Later he moved to Auvers-sur-Oise in northern France, but shot himself in the chest in July 1890.

Les Baux-de-Provence

Les Baux is one of Provence's most popular attractions, so it does get extremely busy. Nonetheless, to miss Les Baux is to miss a unique and stirring sight. In a country of countless fortified towns and villages, it ranks among the finest. Its size alone makes it special. Les Baux occupies a narrow spur of land almost 1km (²/₃ mile) long, flanked by sheer-sided cliffs. But this offshoot of the Alpilles range of hills is not famous simply for its natural attributes.

This protected mini-plateau is the site of a remarkable medieval ghost town. At one time, this citadel was a town of 6,000 inhabitants. Throughout the medieval period, Les Baux and its bellicose independent rulers had a troublesome reputation.

In 1632, the French monarchy's patience finally broke and Les Baux's castle and ramparts were demolished. Its crestfallen population migrated to land reclaimed from the marshes. It then lay forgotten for centuries until the discovery of bauxite – the aluminium ore that takes its name from the town – in the locality in the 19th century.

Nowadays, Les Baux relies on tourism. The lower village, the 'living town', is the focus of all the commercial attention, though it still contains some fine old buildings. Place St-Vincent is a lovely, shady square, with views across to the **Val d'Enfer** (Valley of Hell, so-called because of its weirdly eroded, jagged countenance). Ranged around the square are the 12th-century Église St-Vincent, the 17th-century **Chapelle**

The atmospheric Ville Morte of Les Baux

des **Pénitents-Blancs** and the 16th-century **Hôtel des Porcelets**, which displays works of contemporary art. The **Hôtel de Manville**, a 16th-century building with beautiful Renaissance windows, now serves as the town hall.

Cathédrale d'Images

A short distance northwest of the village on the D27 is the Cathédrale d'Images. Here, the vast caverns of the old bauxite quarries serve as a unique three-dimensional screen for an inventive sound and light show which projects images on to every available surface.

Route de Maillane. Tel: 04 90 54 38 65. www.cathedrale-images.com. Open: Mar & Oct–Jan daily 10am–6pm; Apr–Sept daily 10am–7pm. Open Christmas day and New Year's day 2–6pm. Last entrance 1 hour before closing.

Ville Morte

The undoubted highlight of a visit to Les Baux is the Deserted Village, or Ville Morte. This strange place, on the higher ground to the east and south, is a sprawl of stumpy, intriguing remains that seem to grow out of the bare, dazzlingly white limestone rock. The entire area is sealed off, accessible only through the **Musée Lapidaire** in the lower village (entry by payment). The museum displays artefacts excavated locally together with a presentation of the history of the citadel. On entering the Ville Morte, one of the first sites you come to is the Romanesque Chapelle St-Blaise. From

---

THE PENITENTS

The Middle Ages saw the formation of penitent brotherhoods, mostly charitable organisations patronised by noblemen and even royalty – partly, perhaps, to make a favourable impression through public penance and good deeds and thus massage their consciences; partly to help each other.

Each fraternity had a different-coloured habit and hood, by which they were identified during processions. The White, Grey and Black Penitents all had chapels in Avignon.

In the 16th century both Charles IX and Henri III walked barefoot through Avignon in the white hood that identified the White Penitents.

---

here, walk to the southern tip of the plateau to the monument of the poet Charloun Rieu. Here you can take in an all-encompassing viewpoint south to Arles and the Camargue.

The main defensive sites are at the opposite end of the plateau, beyond the Tour Sarrasine (Saracen Tower). The shell of Les Baux's once mighty castle, demolished in the 17th century, still captures the imagination (there are more magnificent panoramas from its 13th-century keep and the Tour Paravelle).

Château des Baux de Provence. Tel: 04 90 54 55 56. www.chateau-baux-provence.com. Open: spring daily 9am–6.30pm; summer daily 9am–7.30pm; autumn daily 9am–6pm; winter daily 9.30am–5pm. Admission charge.

Les Baux-de-Provence is located on the D27, around 10km (6¼ miles) south of St-Rémy.

The Camargue

The Camargue is unique. This strange, flat, lagoon-like delta is an unfathomable mixture of land and water; it is difficult to discern where land begins and water ends. The Camargue's major feature is the Étang de Vaccarès, a large lagoon that is the focal point for the Parc Naturel Régional de Camargue. The entire area is bounded by two rivers, the Grand and the Petit Rhône, and riddled with irrigation channels, ditches and dikes.

Human settlement is thin on the ground, restricted mainly to the Camargue's hardy *gardians* (herdsmen). However, this indeterminate environment teems with wildlife. The Camargue is home to stick-legged flamingoes, badgers, seabirds and marshbirds, frogs and pond turtles, water snakes and wild boars. To this list is added the famous white horses and the bulls, essential elements in the local Camarguais culture (*see p63*), and another, less appealing member of the local fauna: the mosquito. In summer,

you will need the protection of a potent insect repellent.

Aigues-Mortes

Fortified Aigues-Mortes has a remarkably well-preserved ring of walls. Their survival was due largely to benign neglect, for the town was a forgotten backwater for centuries.

Tour de Constance (Constance Tower) and Ramparts This 13th-century tower is a massive, 40m (131ft) high keep in the northwestern corner of Aigues-Mortes' rectangular fortifications. From the top there is a great view of the town. *Tel: 04 66 53 61 55. Open: Oct–Mar 10am–5.30pm; Apr–Sept 10am–7pm. Ticket office closed 1–2pm and 45 mins before closing time. Admission charge.*

Aigues-Mortes is 42km (26 miles) southwest of Nîmes.

Château d'Avignon

Take a tour of this opulently furnished château, set in beautiful grounds.

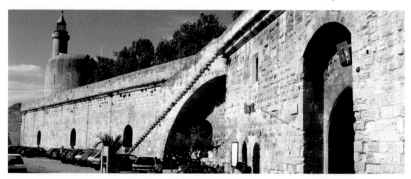

Aigues-Mortes, built as a port, is still largely contained within its 13th-century ramparts

Near Albaron. Tel: 04 90 97 58 58 for information. Open: summer Wed–Mon 10am–5pm. Closed: winter. Admission charge.

La Grande-Motte

La Grande-Motte is a seaside resort of bold triangular apartment blocks, purpose-built in the 1960s and 1970s. Imaginative landscaping makes it less intimidating.

La Grande-Motte is 12km (7 miles) west of Aigues-Mortes.

Maison du Parc

Based alongside the **Étang de Ginès** (Ginès Lagoon), this excellent centre illustrates the Camargue's flora and fauna through exhibitions and real life. There are similar centres – **La Capelière** (*tel: 04 90 97 00 97*) and **Domaine de la Palissade** (*tel: 04 42 86 81 28*) – on the eastern side of Étang de Vaccarès.

*Pont de Gau. Tel: 04 90 97 86 32.
www.parc-camargue.fr.
Open: Apr–Sept daily 10am–6pm;
Oct–Mar daily 9.30am–5.30pm.
Closed: Fri Oct–Mar. Free admission.*

Mas du Pont de Rousty

The **Musée Camarguais** is located at this old *mas* (farmhouse). The museum also has a 3.5km ($2^1/4$-mile) countryside trail.

*On the D570 approximately 9km ($5^1/2$ miles) southwest of Arles.
Tel: 04 90 97 10 82.
Open: Apr–Sept daily 9am–6pm;*

Crane and flamingoes, at home in the watery landscape of the Camargue

*Oct–Mar Wed–Mon 10am–5pm.
Admission charge.*

Parc Ornithologique du Pont de Gau

Alongside the Maison du Parc, this park has aviaries plus many well-signposted trails for bird spotters.

*Tel: 04 90 97 82 62.
www.parcornithologique.com.
Open: Apr–Sept daily 9am–sunset;
Oct–Mar daily 10am–sunset.
Admission charge.*

Stes-Maries-de-la-Mer

This popular seaside resort is too commercialised for some tastes. Its white-painted, boxy dwellings are more reminiscent of Spain than France, an impression reinforced by the flamenco guitarist street musicians. The town is a famous gathering place for the gypsies on 24 and 25 May each year, when they celebrate their patron saint Sarah (*see p15*).

Stes-Maries-de-la-Mer is 33km (21 miles) southeast of Aigues-Mortes.

Tour: The Camargue

The Camargue is a flat, reedy, marshy and watery place. Here, the wildlife takes priority: the prolific bird life, celebrated white horses and bulls, insouciant in their protected habitat, are all visible from the road. A word of advice: theft from cars is particularly rife in this area, so make sure you lock valuables out of sight.

The tour begins at Arles. Allow a full day.

Leave Arles on the D570. This will take you to the Mas du Pont de Rousty, which is a visitor centre for the Parc and will give you a good, all-round introduction to the Camargue. Continue along the D570 to Albaron, turning left along the D37. After 4km (2 1/2 miles), bear right on the C5 for Méjanes.

1 Méjanes

Méjanes is a popular spot with visitors. This large complex offers horse riding,

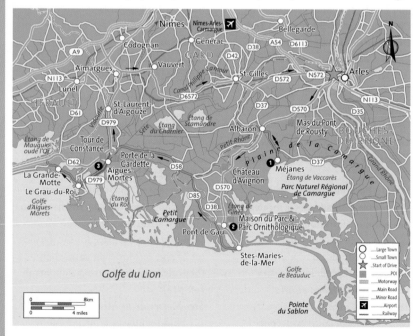

bullfighting (*see box*) and rides on a narrow-gauge railway.

Return to the D570, turning left towards Stes-Maries-de-la-Mer. Shortly, you will come to the entrance to the Château d'Avignon. Continue on to Pont de Gau, stopping off at the Maison du Parc Naturel Régional de Camargue and the next-door Parc Ornithologique.

2 Pont de Gau

At Pont de Gau and along the road into Stes-Maries-de-la-Mer, there are many stables at which you can hire horses. Stes-Maries' best beaches, which stretch for many kilometres, are found to the east of the town, and there is a good choice of boat trips.

Leave Stes-Maries by the D38. Within 6km (4 miles), turn left on to the D85 and cross the Petit Rhône not by bridge but by the flat-bottomed ferry boat, which operates a free shuttle service across the river practically every half-hour during summer (if you are in a hurry, then stay on the D38). The D85 is a quiet back road which gives you an even better chance of seeing the Camargue's wildlife. At the D58, turn left for the walled town of Aigues-Mortes.

3 Aigues-Mortes

Park your car outside the walls and walk through the main gate (still complete with its doors), the Porte de la Gardette. For the best view of the town, which is laid out in an orderly grid pattern, visit the Tour de Constance (Constance Tower) and ramparts.

The distinctive white horses of the Camargue

Le Grau-du-Roi, a bustling little port with a good range of restaurants and gently shelving sandy beach, is along the D979 from Aigues-Mortes. Continue on the coast road to the nearby futuristic resort of La Grande-Motte. Return towards Aigues-Mortes by the inland route, then take the D979 north, turning right on to the N572 for Vauvert and Arles.

HORSES AND BULLS

The Camargue's white horses come from a distinct breed of unknown origin. Together with the black bulls of the region, they are the mainstay of the local Camarguais culture. The horses, bulls and sheep are looked after by *gardians* (local herdsmen). These hardy, proud Camargue-style cowboys play an important role in maintaining the traditions of the area, often working from a simple windowless thatched dwelling known as a *cabane*. The *gardians* are prominent figures in the summer festivals involving bulls and horses. Many towns and villages hold Provençal-style bullfights, in which the bull survives (always check beforehand to confirm details).

Cassis

This is where the Côte d'Azur unofficially begins. Cassis, 22km (14 miles) east of Marseille, is at the start of the most exotic, expensive stretch of coastline in Europe. The little resort, by Riviera standards, is understated and unpretentious.

Visitors come to Cassis for its three small beaches, picturesque harbour and idyllic location. To appreciate this setting to the full, take the spectacular D141 coast road (the route des Crêtes) to La Ciotat and stop off at heart-stopping **Cap Canaille** – at around 400m (1,312ft), reputedly the highest cliff in continental Europe – which looks down directly into the clear blue-green waters of the bay.

Fine buildings line the old port of La Ciotat, a town that once thrived on shipbuilding

Exploring the inaccessible coastline between Marseille and Cassis is not so easy. This strange, fjord-like shore, known as Les Calanques (*see box*), can be viewed by boat from Cassis's harbour.

La Ciotat

Whereas neighbouring Cassis is tucked snugly into its bay, La Ciotat sprawls lazily along a much more open coastline. La Ciotat is a resort of two halves: the old port, sheltering in the lee of Cap de l'Aigle, and a long sandy beach. The old port might not fulfil everyone's expectations: it still displays all the hallmarks of an unglamorous shipbuilding past.

Beyond the café-lined harbour there lies an old town of considerable interest. **Notre-Dame-de-l'Assomption** is a grand 17th-century church overlooking the port, and there are chapels dedicated to the Blue and Black Penitents (*see p59*). History of a more contemporary kind was made in the beach district in 1895, with the first showing of motion pictures by the Lumière brothers.

Musée Ciotaden

This local museum traces the history of the town from ancient times, when it was an outpost of Marseille.
Ancien Hôtel de Ville, quai Ganteaume. Tel: 04 42 71 40 99. www.museeciotaden. org. Open: summer Tue–Sun 4–7pm; winter Tue–Sun 3–6pm. Admission charge.

La Ciotat is on the D559 between Marseille and Toulon.

Fontvieille

Forever associated with this small town at the western approach to the Alpilles is the writer Alphonse Daudet (1840–97). His mainly cheerful, ironic stories make him one of the most important humorists of his time. Daudet's *Lettres de Mon Moulin* (*Letters from my Windmill*) were inspired by this locality. The windmill just south of the town contains a small museum dedicated to him. It stands on a summit that commands an excellent panorama northwards to the vast plain of the Rhône and eastwards to the angular Alpilles. At the foot of the hill there are more Daudet associations – in a museum in the **Château de Montauban**, where Daudet often stayed. (A joint ticket gives admission to the mill and château – details from the Office de Tourisme, *tel: 04 90 54 67 49.*)

Also of interest in this area are the relatively unknown Roman remains a few kilometres south of Fontvieille. The **Aqueducs de Barbegal** are an impressive sight. A long line of ruined archways marks the route of the aqueduct, built to supply Arles with water from Eygalières, 50km (31 miles) away. The remains of a large 4th-century flour mill can also be seen. *Fontvieille is on the D17 about 10km (6 miles) northeast of Arles.*

Marseille

Marseille, more famous for its association with crime, racism and the French Connection films than its

Rugged and remote, the coastline between Marseille and Cassis is best explored by boat

ancient roots, is often bypassed by visitors. Yet it is one of France's largest cities and the capital of Provence. As such, it has a vitality, as well as an ancestry, that demands attention. In any case, Marseille is now trying hard to give itself a new image,

LES CALANQUES

This is the name given to the deeply indented limestone shoreline between Marseille and Cassis, a protected area and haven for wildlife. Arid, rugged and remote, Les Calanques are best explored by boat from Cassis. Calanque de Port-Miou and Calanque de Port-Pin (also accessible by footpath from a signposted car park west of Cassis) are the closest of this series of jutting, jagged inlets. The most memorable is the remoter Calanque d'En-Vau, where towering white cliffs plunge precipitously into the sea.

particularly in anticipation of its status as European Capital of Culture in 2013. Major infrastructure improvements are underway (a tram system was opened in 2007, for instance) and the city is encouraging the building of new, high-quality hotels. A key project is the redevelopment of the area around the docks as 'Euroméditerranée' – with buildings designed by leading architects, such as Zaha Hadid and Jean Nouvel.

Very little remains of the Greek harbour colony of Massalia, founded in the 6th century BC. From Roman maritime base to the docklands and refineries of the 19th and 20th centuries, it has always been the port that has determined Marseille's cosmopolitan personality. The Vieux Port is as sunny and animated as any southern city. Leading from the quayside is the famous La Canebière, lined with cafés and shops.

Marseille's City pass allows entry to 14 museums, and travel on public transport. *Visit the tourist office (4 La Canebière. Tel: 04 91 13 89 00) or www.marseille-tourisme.com for more information.*

Abbaye St-Victor
Marseille's oldest church has a crypt containing a 5th-century sepulchre. *Place St-Victor.*

Basilique de Notre-Dame-de-la-Garde
The steep climb to this 19th-century Romano-Byzantine church is worth it for the wonderful panoramas alone. *On an outcrop high above the port; head uphill and pick up the boulevard André Aune off rue/ boulevard Fort Notre-Dame running from the quay.*

Cathédrale de la Major
The giant 19th-century neo-Byzantine cathedral dwarfs its ancient harbinger, the Romanesque Major Ancienne. *Along avenue Robert Schuman.*

Château d'If
This craggy island-fortress, like San Francisco's Alcatraz, was used as a prison for centuries (Edmond Dantès, hero of Alexandre Dumas's *The Count of Monte Cristo*, was incarcerated here). *Visits by boat from quai des Belges. Tel: 04 91 46 54 65. Open: May–Sept daily 9.30am–6.30pm; Oct–Apr*

The craggy fortress of Château d'If

9am–5.30pm (closed Mon Sept–Mar).
Admission charge.

Musée des Beaux-Arts
(Museum of Fine Arts)

Art from the 16th to 19th centuries is
displayed here.
Palais Longchamp. Tel: 04 91 14 59 30.
Open: Jun–Sept Tue–Sun 11am–6pm;
Oct–May Tue–Sun 10am–5pm. Admission
charge, except on Sun morning.

Musée Cantini

20th-century paintings and sculptures.
19 rue Grignan. Tel: 04 91 54 77 75.
Open: Jun–Sept Tue–Sun 11am–6pm;
Oct–May Tue–Sun 10am–5pm.
Admission charge.

Musée des Docks Romains

The museum contains remains of a rare
Roman warehouse plus other artefacts.
Place Vivaux. Tel: 04 91 91 24 62.
Open: Jun–Sept Tue–Sun 11am–6pm;
Oct–May Tue–Sun 10am–5pm.
Admission charge.

Musée Grobet-Labadié

Displays the extensive private collection
of Louis Grobet and Marie-Louise
Labadié.
140 boulevard Longchamp. Tel: 04 91 62
21 82. Open: Jun–Sept Tue–Sun
11am–6pm; Oct–May Tue–Sun
10am–5pm. Admission charge.

Musée d'Histoire de Marseille

Covering prehistory to the Gallo-Roman
period, the most famous exhibit here is

The many-domed Cathédrale de la Major

an exceptionally well-preserved wreck of
a Roman merchant vessel.
Centre Bourse. Tel: 04 91 90 42 22.
Open: Mon–Sat noon–7pm.
Admission charge.

Musée du Vieux Marseille
Maison Diamantée

This museum of social history is based
at the 16th-century Maison Diamantée.
2 rue de la Prison. Tel: 04 91 55 28 68.
Open: Jun–Sept Tue–Sun 11am–6pm;
Oct–May Tue–Sun 10am–5pm.
Admission charge.

La Vieille Charité

A restored 17th-century hospice,
designed by Pierre Puget, Vieille
Charité's contemporary role is as a
centre for the arts and science.
Exhibitions and special events are
held here, and it is home to the
excellent **Musée d'Archéologie
Méditerranéenne**.
2 rue de la Charité. Tel: 04 91 14 58 58.
Open: Jun–Sept daily 11am–6pm;
Oct–May daily 10am–5pm.
Admission charge.

Bouches-du-Rhône

Walk: Marseille

Marseille is a big city, but don't be intimidated. This is a city which walkers can quite easily get to grips with (after finding a place to park!). The Vieux Port (Old Port) is Marseille's birthplace and remains its vibrant heart. Belying the images of a dark-alleyed, slightly sinister city riddled with crime, this part of Marseille is inherently Mediterranean, colourful and exceedingly photogenic.

Allow a day for the walk.

From the Office de Tourisme at 4 La Canebière, walk down to quai des Belges.

1 Quai des Belges

Quai des Belges looks out across the Vieux Port, which was discovered by the Phoenicians in 600 BC. Tiered, pastel-shaded houses and grand buildings line the quayside, which is the venue for the morning fish market.

Above the large harbour, which bristles with a forest of yacht masts, is the enormous neo-Byzantine Basilique de Notre-Dame-de-la-Garde, which looks out over the scene from a 162m (531ft) high limestone outcrop.

Quai du Port leads to the handsome **Hôtel de Ville**, which is a fine example of 17th-century Baroque Provençal architecture.

Turn right here along rue de la Prison for the Musée du Vieux Marseille (Museum of Old Marseille) housed in the 16th-century Maison Diamantée. Close by, along rue du Lacydon at place Vivaux, is the Musée des Docks Romains.

Retrace your steps a short way along rue de Lacydon and climb the steps to rue Caisserie, crossing the road to climb a much narrower, historic staircase, montée des Accoules.

2 Montée des Accoules

Montée des Accoules takes you into Le Panier, the oldest part of Marseille. Much of Le Panier was destroyed by the Nazis during World War II. On the hilly slopes above the Vieux Port, the surviving section – a rabbit warren of claustrophobic, narrow streets and alleyways hemmed in by tall buildings – preserves an authentic atmosphere of Marseille as it once was.

Montée des Accoules leads to place de Lenche, where you turn right along rue de l'Évêché, then left along rue Four du Chapitre towards the waterfront and the Cathédrale de la Major. Proceed along avenue Robert Schuman, turning right into rue Antoine-Becker, left along rue de l'Évêché, right into place Francis Chirat, and right again into rue de l'Observance.

The large building on your left is la Vieille Charité (Old Charity Cultural Centre), the entrance to which is off rue de la Charité (turn left at the end of rue de l'Observance).

From rue de la Charité turn right into rue Puits du Denier, then right into rue du Panier. Rue des Moulins leads to the pleasant, tree-lined place des Moulins, and once more on to montée des Accoules. Walk back down the steps, turning left into rue Caisserie, then on to Grand'Rue, crossing over rue de la République – one of the city's main streets – to the Jardin des Vestiges (Garden of Ruins).

3 Jardin des Vestiges

You can take a well-earned rest in this attractive sunken garden, excavated to reveal the fortifications of the original Greek town that existed here, Massalia, the 1st-century docks and the 3rd-century entrance.

The **Musée d'Histoire de Marseille** (*open: Mon–Sat noon–7pm*) is located here, part of the huge Centre Bourse shopping complex.

From the garden, follow rue Henri Barbusse to rue Reine Élisabeth, cross La Canebière, then keep on rue Paradis till it crosses rue Grignan. Musée Cantini will be on your left.

Marseille

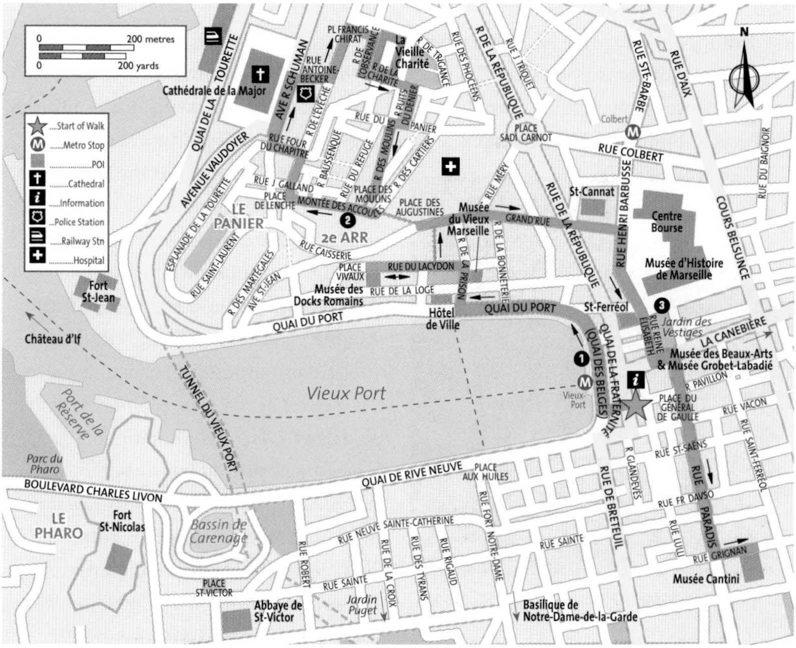

Nîmes

Denim originated in the textile mills of Nîmes (de Nîmes: denim). Despite the ubiquity of the cloth, the city is more famous as a place of great antiquity, exemplified by its outstandingly well-preserved Arènes (Roman amphitheatre). In recent years Nîmes has attracted much attention for its bold – and sometimes controversial – experiments in urban regeneration with notable modern buildings such as the Carrée d'Art. While there is still some way to go (parts of the city are still in need of care and attention), Nîmes has become a fascinating place for lovers of architecture and art old and new.

Arènes (Roman Amphitheatre)

This vast amphitheatre, dating from the 1st century and one of the best preserved in the whole of the Roman world, is still in regular use for everything from pop concerts to bullfights. Its two-storey façade encloses a complex building of galleries, vaulted passageways and tiered terraces that can accommodate over 20,000 people. Other Roman sites in Nîmes include the **Porte Auguste** (Augustus's Gate) and **Castellum** (a water tower), a short distance northeast and northwest of the centre respectively.
Boulevard des Arènes. Tel: 04 66 21 82 56. Open: summer daily 9.30am–6.30pm; winter daily 10am–5pm. Closed: during public events. Admission charge.

Cathédrale Notre-Dame et St-Castor

Although dating from 1096, it has been almost totally remodelled and rebuilt over the centuries. Note the preserved frieze in the west front, which depicts scenes from the Old Testament.
Place aux Herbes.

Jardin de la Fontaine

This delightful garden is, for many, the highlight of their visit to Nîmes. Created in 1750 around the spring that gave Nîmes its existence, it is France's oldest public garden, set against a backdrop of rocky, wooded slopes. On the slopes above stands the **Tour Magne**, a 34m (112ft) high Roman tower commanding spectacular views.
Northwest of city centre. Open: Gardens mid-Sept–Mar daily 7.30am–6.30pm; Apr–mid-Sept 7.30am–sunset. Free admission. Tour Magne: Nov–Feb daily 9.30am–1pm & 2–4.30pm; Mar & Oct daily 9.30am–1pm & 2–6pm; Apr, May & Sept daily 9.30am–6.30pm, Jun–Aug daily 10am–8pm. Admission charge.

The Maison Carrée: a Roman temple in Greek style

A fountain in the Jardin de la Fontaine

Maison Carrée

This colonnaded Roman temple ('The Square House') is unique for its state of preservation, which belies its age of nearly 2,000 years. Its purity of line and harmonious proportions make it one of the finest temples in the Greek tradition outside Italy. Works of art are currently displayed here.

Place de la Maison Carrée. Tel: 04 66 21 82 56. Open: Oct–Feb daily 10am–1pm & 2–5pm (6.30pm in Oct); Mar daily 10am–6.30pm; Apr, May & Sept daily 10am–7pm; Jun–Aug daily 10am–8pm. Free admission.

Musée Archéologique

Displays a range of Roman artefacts. The **Musée d'Histoire Naturelle et de Préhistoire** (Museum of Natural History and Prehistory – *tel: 04 66 67 39 14*) is housed at the same address.

13 bis boulevard Amiral-Courbet.

Tel: 04 66 76 74 80. Open: Tue–Sun 10am–6pm. Admission charge.

Musée des Beaux-Arts

The gallery has a large Roman mosaic, paintings of the French, Italian, Flemish and Dutch schools from the 15th to mid-19th centuries, and modern art.

Rue de la Cité Foulc. Tel: 04 66 67 38 21. Open: Tue–Sun 10am–6pm. Admission charge.

Musée du Vieux Nîmes (Museum of Old Nîmes)

The museum contains an interesting selection of Provençal and Languedocian furniture, pottery, painting and everyday objects.

Place aux Herbes. Tel: 04 66 76 73 70. Open: Tue–Sun 10am–6pm. Free admission.

Nîmes is 45km (28 miles) southwest of Avignon, just off the A9.

Walk: Nîmes

Nîmes has an unexpected variety of faces – part elegant, part shabby, part historic, part futuristic. The creation of a conservation zone in 1985 has led to the rejuvenation of old Nîmes. Conveniently for those on foot, most of the main sites are concentrated in and around this central area.

Allow at least half a day for the walk.

From the Office de Tourisme at 6 rue Auguste (tel: 04 66 58 38 00; www.ot-nimes.fr), walk a short distance south to the Maison Carrée.

1 Maison Carrée

Along with the Arènes (Roman amphitheatre), this Roman temple is Nîmes' most famous landmark. Across the open space from Maison Carrée lies an architectural counterpoint in the form of a modern – and controversial – building of typically bold, uncompromising design. This is the **Carrée d'Art** (*tel: 04 66 76 35 70; open: Tue–Sun 10am–6pm*), the work of British architect Sir Norman Foster. Intended as a Pompidou Centre of the south, it serves as an art gallery and library. Its central atrium is designed to evoke the interior courtyards of Nîmes houses.

Walk south along boulevard Victor-Hugo, visiting Église St-Paul, built in the 19th century in Romano-Byzantine style. Take rue de la Monnaie to place du Marché.

2 Place du Marché

Place du Marché is the scene of Nîmes' medieval corn market. The charming modern marble and bronze fountain with a crocodile echoes the city's crest.

Leave the place by rue de la Fresque, a road lined with historic houses. Turn right into rue de Bernis and right again along rue de l'Aspic, a busy shopping street. Turn left into rue de l'Hôtel de Ville. The 15th-century archway beside the Hôtel de Ville leads to rue de la Trésorerie. Turn right into rue Dorée, another street lined with historic but dilapidated houses. At Grand Rue, turn left.

3 Chapelle des Jésuites

The 17th-century former Jesuit Chapel along Grand Rue is one of a number of sites in Nîmes that demonstrate the imaginative, forward-thinking attitude of the city authorities. It is now used for cultural events, and in summer its cool, spacious interior becomes an exhibition area for works of modern art.

Turn left into rue du Chapitre.

4 Hôtel de Régis

The Hôtel de Régis at 14 rue du Chapitre is another of the city's many fine old dwellings. An 18th-century façade with a carved entranceway leads into a magnificent cobbled courtyard (16th-century) with Roman artefacts.

Turn right along rue des Marchands for the pretty place aux Herbes and the Cathédrale Notre-Dame et St-Castor, together with its neighbour, the Musée du Vieux Nîmes. Along rue de la Madeleine, take a short detour down ruelle Ste-Eugénie to see the Église Ste-Eugénie, the oldest church in the city. From rue de la Madeleine, turn left into rue de l'Aspic, which leads south to the Arènes (Roman amphitheatre).

5 Esplanade Charles de Gaulle

The Esplanade beyond the Arènes is a pleasant place to end the walk. Its 1848 **Fontaine Pradier** (named after its sculptor) depicts a female figure who symbolises Nîmes. The grand **Palais de Justice** (Law Courts), in neoclassical style, stands on one side of the Esplanade.

Nîmes

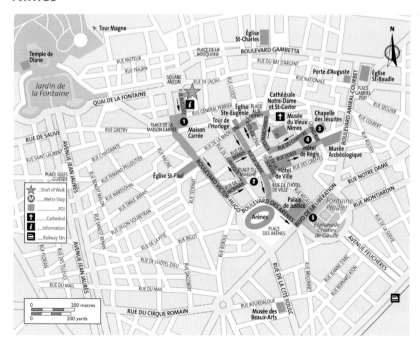

Pont du Gard

This 275m (902ft) long Roman aqueduct was constructed in the 1st century to span the Gardon Valley. It was the crowning glory of a 50km (31-mile) system of tunnels, ditches, water-regulating basins and other bridges, built to carry water from Uzès to Nîmes. The construction of the Pont du Gard represented a truly monumental feat of engineering. Giant blocks of dressed stone were hoisted and then slotted into place without mortar. Built in three tiers, it has 35 arches along the top directly below the water channel – still visible where covering stones are missing – 11 arches in the middle, and six at the bottom (surprisingly, only one of these bottom arches actually spans the river). The structure towers nearly 50m (164ft) above the waters of the Gardon, yet possesses a sense of harmony that modern bridge builders seem incapable of replicating. A road

built in the 17th century along the east side of the bottom tier carries traffic, forming part of the minor road D981. But the Pont du Gard's really miraculous feature is its state of preservation. Its weathered golden stonework looks set to last for another 2,000 years.

Increasing numbers of visitors threaten the conservation of this important site. To raise awareness of the bridge's illustrious past, an interesting information centre-cum-museum has been structured outlining its history, and explaining the aqueduct's route and function, and includes a section of exhibits as well as a short film designed with children in mind. The parkland grounds, strewn with Roman remains, prove popular for picnics, although there is a café and a restaurant; there is also a souvenir shop. The whole area is accessible free of charge but the two car parks have fixed opening hours.
Tel: 08 20 90 33 30. www.pontdugard.fr.

The moss-covered fountain near the Porte de l'Horloge in Salon-de-Provence

NOSTRADAMUS 1503–66

Nostradamus was born Michel de Nostre Dame in St-Rémy – to Jewish parents. As with most Jews in southern France, they had been forced by the Inquisition to espouse the Catholic faith. As a student, he devoted much time to languages and science, attending the University of Avignon, where he studied liberal arts, and the University of Montpellier, where he qualified as a doctor.

Nostradamus lost his first wife and two children to the plague – despite having found a remedy for the disease – and, distraught, he travelled France and Italy for six years. In 1547 he settled in Salon-de-Provence and remarried. Over the years he garnered a reputation as something of a prophet and wrote his famous *Les Centuries*, a series of theses and predictions. A decade later he was appointed Royal Physician to Charles IX and two years later died in his sleep.

Parking open: 6am–1am. The various cultural activities are closed Mon. Admission charge for parking.

Salon-de-Provence

Salon's medieval centre, huddling beneath a rocky hill crowned by the Château de l'Empéri, has seen quite a few changes of late. French architects and town planners have been mostly successful in rejuvenating the heart of the town. New apartments rub shoulders with renovated 16th-century houses, smart shops are beginning to appear in the maze of old streets, and the 13th-century Église St-Michel is having a face-lift. Mercifully, Salon has not been emasculated by this modern development, save at the foot of the château in the place des Centuries,

which is unfortunately a hopeless open space devoid of life.

Elsewhere, Salon has much to delight the eye. The 18th-century mossy fountain outside the Porte de l'Horloge gateway resembles a giant green toadstool. Along the rue de l'Horloge there is a huge mural featuring Michel de Nostradamus (1503–66), the physician/astrologer who spent the last 19 years of his life here (*see box*). A statue to civil engineer Adam de Craponne (1527–76), whose canal brought water to this previously arid region, stands outside the splendid 17th-century Hôtel de Ville (Town Hall).

Château/Musée de l'Empéri

A military museum of the French armies from Louis XIV to 1914 is housed in the massive castle.
Montée de Puech. Tel: 04 90 44 72 80. Open: Wed–Mon 10am–noon & 2–6pm. Admission charge.

Musée Grevin de la Provence

The history and legends of Provence are imaginatively presented here.
Place des Centuries. Tel: 04 90 56 36 30. Open: 9am–noon & 2–6pm. Closed: Sat & Sun morning. Admission charge.

Musée de Nostradamus

A museum devoted to Nostradamus's work in the house where this fascinating man lived.
11 rue Nostradamus. Tel: 04 90 56 64 31. Open: as for Musée Grevin. Admission charge.

Les Antiques near St-Rémy-de-Provence

Musée du Savon et de Marseille

A historical journey into the origins of Provence's famous Marseille soap.
148 avenue Paul-Bourret. Tel: 04 90 53 24 77. www.marius-fabre.fr. Open: Mon–Fri 9.30–11.30am & 2–5pm (until 4pm on Fri). Admission charge.

Salon-de-Provence is 53km (33 miles) northwest of Marseille.

St-Rémy-de-Provence

St-Rémy is another famous Roman town. Les Antiques – a generic name covering St-Rémy's outstanding commemorative arch and mausoleum – stand side by side a short distance south of the town on the D5 to Les Baux. The arch signalled the entrance to Glanum, one of the most significant ancient sites in France.

The historic centre of St-Rémy itself is compact, charming and self-contained. Nostradamus was born along rue Hoche in 1503. Vincent Van Gogh's time in St-Rémy is remembered in the Centre d'Art in the Hôtel Estrine. During his 12-month stay at the St-Paul-de-Mausole psychiatric clinic near Les Antiques, he painted around 150 canvases, including some of his most famous paintings, such as *The Starry Night* and *Wheat Field with Cypress*. The building, originally a 12th-century monastery, is still a clinic. Around its grounds (and in other parts of St-Rémy) you can see reproductions of some of Van Gogh's paintings at the vantage points from which he probably painted them.
Tel: 04 90 92 77 00. Church and cloisters open: Apr–Sept daily 9.30am–7pm; Oct–Mar daily 10.15am–5pm. Admission charge.

Les Antiques

Both monuments are located on the roadside. The triumphal arch is decorated with beautiful Greek-influenced carvings celebrating the Roman conquest of Marseille. Next to it is one of the world's best-preserved Roman structures, still standing at its full 18m (59ft). Previously known as a mausoleum, it is now thought to have been a monument to Lucius and Gaius Caesar.
2km (1¼ miles) south of the town centre along avenue Vincent-Van-Gogh. Free admission.

Centre d'Art Présence Van Gogh

Changing exhibitions of modern works plus a permanent display of reproductions of Van Gogh's works can be seen in the beautiful 18th-century Hôtel Estrine.
8 rue Estrine. Tel: 04 90 92 34 72. Open: mid-Mar, Apr & Oct–Nov Tue–

Sun 10.30am–12.30pm & 2–6pm;
May–Sept Tue–Sun 10am–12.30pm &
2–7pm. Admission charge.

Glanum

When Glanum was excavated from
1921 onwards, it revealed evidence of
neolithic settlement. Later, in the 2nd
century BC, a Gallo-Greek town was
established here. But what we see today
is mainly Roman, more or less spanning
the 1st to 3rd centuries AD. Glanum was
an army base, spa town and important
crossroads for two major routes between
Italy and Spain. The extensive ruins
provide a wonderful insight into the life
of a thriving Roman city and include
temples, a forum and thermal baths.
2km (1 1/4 miles) south of the town centre
along avenue Vincent-Van-Gogh.
Tel: 04 90 92 23 79. Open: Apr–Aug daily
10am–6.30pm; Sept–Mar Tue–Sun
10.30am–5pm. Last admission 45 minutes
before closing. Admission charge.

Musée des Alpilles

Well-presented displays focus mainly
on folk culture and local traditions.
Place Favier. Tel: 04 90 92 68 24.
Open: Jan–Feb & Nov–Dec Tue–Sat
2–5pm; Mar–Jun & Sept–Oct Tue–Sat
10am–noon & 2–6pm; Jul & Aug
Tue–Sat 10am–12.30pm & 2–7pm.
Admission charge.

Musée Archéologique

Glanum's excavated artefacts are
exhibited in this impressive house,
once home of the Sade family.

GOOD KING RENÉ

A scholar and artist, 'le bon roi' René d'Anjou
ruled Provence from its capital, Aix, and his
impregnable castle at Tarascon. After losing
Anjou to the King of France, he settled in
Provence in 1434, dying 46 years later in 1480.
He was king in name only of Hungary,
Jerusalem and Naples. His rule in Provence
was a period of great cultural expansion.
René's father, Louis II d'Anjou, had founded
the University of Aix and in his mould René
continued nurturing an interest in the arts
and in true Renaissance style encouraged
their patronage.

Hôtel de Sade, 1 rue de Parage. Tel: 04 90
92 64 04. Closed for restoration until
2012. Admission charge.

St-Rémy-de-Provence is 40km (25 miles)
northwest of Salon-de-Provence.

Tarascon

This town on the banks of the Rhône
boasts a splendid fairy-tale castle, the
Château du Roi René (*see box*), one of
the best-preserved 15th-century castles
in France. It faces the castle at Beaucaire
on the opposite bank.

Château du Roi René

Impregnable defences protect a
surprisingly decorative and luxurious
interior.
Boulevard du Roi René. Tel: 04 90 91 01
93. Open: Apr–Sept daily 10am–6.30pm;
Oct–Mar Tue–Sun 10.30am–5pm.
Admission charge.

Tarascon is about 16km (10 miles) west
of St-Rémy-de-Provence.

Var

The Riviera proper starts within this département. *Away from the main resort areas, the rugged coastlines fringing the forested Massif des Maures and Massif de l'Estérel still preserve their natural beauty. Inland, thickly wooded hills rise into the Haut-Var, a huge expanse of bare plateaux and deserted uplands.*

Aups

At an altitude of over 500m (1,640ft), Aups is traditionally regarded as the start of the Alps. Perched in the the Haut-Var, this peaceful little town preserves an authentic atmosphere. Markets (selling local produce such as honey, olive oil and goats' cheese) are held on Wednesday and Saturday in the square beside the Hôtel de Ville (Town

Var

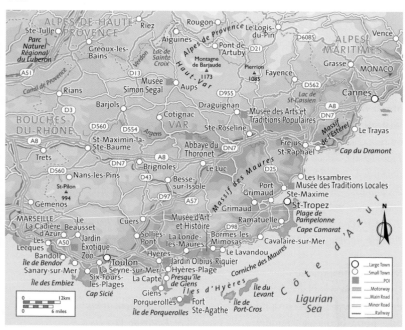

Var

Bandol, with its marina, casino and villas, is the epitome of Côte d'Azur style

Hall). In winter Aups is famed for its truffles. There is much to appreciate in Aups's unspoilt, leafy old streets: the many fountains, the renovated doorway to the Église St-Pancrace, the remains of a town gate and ramparts at the far end of rue des Aires.

Musée Simon Segal
This small gallery, in an old Ursuline convent, displays works by Russian-born painter Simon Segal and other modern artists. There is also a small museum commemorating the World War II Resistance.
Avenue Albert-1er. Tel: 04 94 70 01 95. Open: Jul & Aug Wed–Mon 10am–noon & 4–7pm. Admission charge.

Aups is 29km (18 miles) northwest of Draguignan.

Bandol
Bandol has all the attributes of a stylish Côte d'Azur resort: the palm trees, the beaches, the casino, the marina. The

resort has another asset – the **Île de Bendor,** owned by the family of the late *pastis* magnate Paul Ricard. The small island, accessible by a frequent boat service, contains a diving school, arts and conference centres, and a museum dedicated to wines and spirits.
The local wine is among the finest in Provence.

Bandol's neighbouring resort, the less flashy **Sanary-sur-Mer** also offers boat trips – in this case, to the larger **Île des Embiez**.

Jardin Exotique Zoo
This tropical garden and zoo is a popular attraction.
Located near the autoroute exit for Bandol. Tel: 04 94 29 40 38. www. zoosanary.com. Open: daily 8am–noon (10am–noon Sun) & 2–7pm (until 6pm in winter). Closed: Sun mornings in winter. Admission charge.

Bandol is about 16km (10 miles) west of Toulon.

View of the old town, Bormes-les-Mimosas

Bormes-les-Mimosas

You can forgive the locals for embellishing the name of this hilltop village, originally known simply as Bormes and rechristened Bormes-les-Mimosas in 1968. There are flowers everywhere, in baskets, urns, tubs, pots and window boxes, climbing up the fronts of the houses, and in immaculately tended flowerbeds.

The part of Bormes that attracts visitors – the Vieux Village (Old Village) – is perched at the top of a steep, south-facing slope, with wonderful views of nearby Le Lavandou and the coast. The alleyways and narrow streets can be explored by following a waymarked **Circuit Touristique** with numbered stopping-off places (details from the tourist office, *tel: 04 94 01 38 38; www.bormeslesmimosas.com*). Bormes is almost too perfect: the street names are a little fanciful – montée du Paradis, for

instance – and there are even special slatted cubbyholes in which to hide the dustbins!

Musée d'Art et Histoire

Bormes's history, together with the work of local artist Jean-Charles Cazin (1841–1901), are the main themes here. *65 rue Carnot. Tel: 04 94 71 56 60. Open: Oct–May Tue–Sat 10am–noon & 2–5.30pm; Jun–Sept Tue–Sat 10am–noon, 3–6.30pm. Closed: Wed morning and Sun afternoon. Admission charge.*

Bormes-les-Mimosas is off the D559 about 22km (14 miles) east of Hyères.

Draguignan

This large town stands at the gateway to the high country of the Haut-Var. There is not a great deal to distract visitors passing through on the way to the Grand Canyon du Verdon. The most attractive part of the town is the medieval quarter around the place du Marché, the Tour de l'Horloge (a fine 17th-century clock tower) and the Église St-Michel, guarded by ancient gateways.

Musée des Arts et Traditions Populaires

Exhibits include traditional costumes, agricultural implements and a Provençal kitchen.

15 rue Joseph-Roumanille.
Tel: 04 94 47 05 72. Open: 9am–noon &
2–6pm. Closed: Sun morning & Mon.
Admission charge.

Draguignan is 30km (19 miles) northwest of Fréjus.

Fréjus/St-Raphaël

Fréjus is a place of many parts, and blends into its more fashionable neighbour, St-Raphaël. Most visitors come for the beach, **Fréjus-Plage**, at the western end of this sprawling coastal town. In the east there is a smart new marina and harbour complex, while beyond that a long, sandy beach ends at St Raphaël's attractive harbour and seafront casino.

The town of Fréjus itself, 1km ($^2/_3$ mile) or so inland, is noted for its Roman remains. **Forum Julii** was a large Roman town and port: too large, perhaps, for us to appreciate fully today, since vestiges of Roman occupation are scattered across a wide area, making it difficult to build up any coherent picture. Beside the N7 into town from the northeast are ruined arches from a 40km (25-mile) aqueduct system. An open-air theatre (still used for concerts) stands incongruously among quiet suburbs along avenue du Théâtre-Romain, while the Arènes (amphitheatre) lies beyond the Porte des Gaules gateway in the west of the town. Medieval Fréjus's centrepiece is the Cathedral Close, a collection of important religious buildings dating back to early Christian times.

Var

A boat leaving St-Raphaël harbour

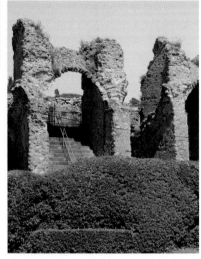

The Arènes at Fréjus

Arènes (Amphitheatre)

Although not as impressive as others in Provence, it is still used for concerts and bullfights.
Rue Henri-Vadon. Tel: 04 94 51 34 31. Open: winter Tue–Sun 9.30am–12.30pm & 2–5pm; summer Tue–Sun 9.30am–12.30pm & 2–6pm. Admission charge.

Cathedral Close

The well-preserved baptistery stands next to an impressive 10th- to 13th-century cathedral built in an austere early Provençal style. Lighter in effect are its slender-columned cloisters, enclosing a delightful little garden. An archaeological museum is also located here.
Place Formigé. Tel: 04 94 51 26 30. Cathedral open: mornings &

2.30–6.30pm. Free admission. Baptistery, cloisters and museum open: winter Tue–Sun 9am–noon & 2–5pm; summer daily 9am–6.30pm. Admission charge.

Fréjus is 37km (23 miles) north of St-Tropez.

Hyères

Miraculously, the town of Hyères has avoided the worst excesses of Côte tourism, possibly because of its location a short distance inland (the coast has receded since medieval times, when Hyères served as a port for the Crusades). Even the 'new' Hyères of the 19th century, which covers the hill on the approach to the old town, has preserved its original decorum. This area, with its wide streets, waving palm trees, gardens, grand villas and casino, retains the character of its *belle époque* when it rivalled Nice as a fashionable resort for the rich and famous (Queen Victoria stayed here once).

The Vieille Ville (Old Town) of medieval Hyères lies beyond the ancient gateway at place Georges-Clemenceau. Suddenly, you are among the narrow, typically claustrophobic streets of a real French town in which real people live and work. Place Massillon, venue of a daily market, is a delightful little self-contained Provençal square surrounded by tall buildings and unglamorous cafés. It is overlooked by the Tour St-Blaise, a 12th-century tower of the Knights Templar.

The Vieille Ville's main church, the imposing 13th-century Église St-Louis, is on place de la République east of place Massillon. High on the hill in place St-Paul stands Collégiale St-Paul, a former collegiate church attached by archway to a Renaissance house with a fairy-tale conical turret (the church is open afternoons, except Monday). Place St-Paul, a magnificent viewpoint 5km (3 miles) from the sea, looks out past the spit of land known as Presqu'île de Giens to the Îles d'Hyères. You can climb yet further up the hill to the flower-filled Parc St-Bernard and a ruined château.

The opening-up of Toulon Hyères airport to international flights has made the town more accessible to foreign visitors.

Hyères's beaches lie to the south, along Hyères-Plage and the 5km (3-mile) long Presqu'île de Giens.

Jardin Olbius-Riquier

This attractive garden, south of the town, contains a lake, children's play area, aviaries, a profusion of exotic plants and a small zoo.

Avenue Ambroise-Thomas. Tel: 04 94 00 78 65. Open: summer daily 7.30am–8pm; winter daily 7.30am–5pm. Free admission.

Site Olbia

Greek and Roman finds from local excavations are on display, together with paintings and items of natural history.

Quartier de l'Almanarre. Tel: 04 94 57 98 28. Open: May–Sept Tue & Sat 3–6pm, Thur & Fri 9.30am–12.30pm & 3–6pm. Admission charge.

Hyères is 82km (50 miles) southeast of Marseille off the A570.

Îles d'Hyères

Boats for the islands of Porquerolles, Port-Cros and Le Levant – also known as the Îles d'Or (Golden Isles) – depart daily all year round from Port d'Hyères,

The 12th-century Tour St-Blaise dominates Hyères's market square

next to Hyères-Plage. A few kilometres east of Hyères, **La Londe-les-Maures/Port-de-Miramar** has daily boat trips from mid-June to mid-September. One-way journeys last from 30–90 minutes depending on port of departure, with shorter times from La Londe.

The nearest and largest of these islands, Porquerolles, is predictably the most developed, though everything is on a small scale. You can walk or cycle (bikes can be rented locally) through a landscape of pine trees, eucalyptus and heather to some beautiful sandy beaches. Fort Ste-Agathe, a stronghold overlooking the village, has a small museum. The Île de Port-Cros, more or less uninhabited, and the smallest national park in France, is a thickly vegetated haven that supports a wealth of wildlife. The Île du Levant, the furthest of the three islands from Hyères, is mainly a military base.
Office de Tourisme, Forum du Casino, 3 ave Ambroise Thomas, 83400 Hyères Cedex. Tel: 04 94 01 84 50. www.hyeres-tourisme.com

Le Lavandou

Travelling eastwards along the coast, you will begin to sense the presence of first-division glamour – and serious money – on reaching Le Lavandou. This is another fishing village that has become a glittering haven for holiday yachts. Not as densely developed as many of its contemporaries, it boasts a fine, spacious sandy beach and an animated harbour. Boats leave from the harbour for the Îles d'Hyères. The coast road east winds its way along the mountain-backed Corniche des Maures to St-Tropez.
Le Lavandou is 23km (14 1/4 miles) east of Hyères.

St-Tropez

Though it can be hectic in high summer, come in the quieter months and you immediately appreciate why St-Tropez has cast a spell over so many – from Matisse to Brigitte Bardot.

After all the hype, St-Tropez's diminutive size comes as quite a surprise. The Vieux Port (Old Port) is the heart of St-Tropez. It is here that the multi-millionaires moor their huge yachts. It is here that the merely rich come to parade. And it is here that the *petit bourgeoisie* come to gawp at the ostentatious displays of wealth.

Behind the Vieux Port lies a picturesque town and the rue de la Citadelle, which leads to a high bluff dominated by a 16th-century fortress.

St-Tropez's beach area lies a few kilometres to the south. The **Plage de Pampelonne**, although it has 5km (3 miles) of sand, becomes exceedingly busy in summer. Further south again, around Cape Camarat, there is a better chance of finding a quieter spot along the Plage de l'Escalet. There is also a small beach, the Plages des Graniers, in walking distance from the centre of St-Tropez, just beyond the Citadelle, and the town's cemetery.

The high life

The Riviera has long been a playground of the wealthy, the very name conjuring up images of 24-carat lifestyles involving luxury yachts, palatial hotels, bougainvillaea-draped villas, private beaches and spinning roulette wheels.

It was not always so. When the English novelist Tobias Smollett sought a cure for his bronchitis in Nice in 1764, he wrote of a land of 'rude peasants and persistent mosquitoes', though he did find the climate to his taste. Another Englishman, Lord Brougham – the Lord Chancellor, no less – found it even more to his liking 90 years later, when an enforced stay in the tiny fishing village of Cannes proved far more agreeable than he had expected. Within a decade, so many of his compatriots were travelling south for the winter that

Nice had a Promenade des Anglais (Promenade of the English). By the end of the 19th century, the Riviera was playing host to Queen Victoria and the crowned heads of Italy, Sweden, Bulgaria and Belgium, as well as Grand Dukes of Russia and the Shah of Persia. 'Princes, princes, nothing but princes,' grumbled that master of the short story, Guy de Maupassant.

The clientele changed with the social upheaval that followed World War I. Newly rich Americans swarmed in with their taste for high living, making the Riviera a symbol of the Jazz Age and, increasingly, a summer destination. It was here that Gabrielle 'Coco' Chanel – perfumer and fashion designer – made sunbathing chic, and nowhere did the Roaring Twenties roar more excitingly. The area's seal of fashionable approval was again renewed when film star Grace Kelly came here to marry Prince Rainier.

Today the Côte d'Azur is as siren-like as ever, despite the dangers of being swamped by its own success. Movie stars, millionaires, pop singers, successful writers – all fall victim to the allure of sunshine, sybaritic living and the swank that comes with a yearning for the high life.

All the best boats moor in the high-society harbour in Monaco

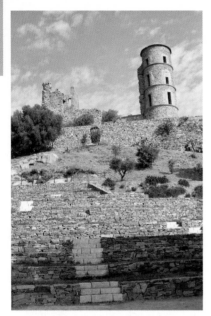

A ruined château overlooks picturesque Grimaud village

At the approach to the St-Tropez peninsula is **Port Grimaud**. Reclaimed from marshland in the 1960s, it is a mostly successful attempt to create the look of a traditional fishing village in the modern idiom. Inland is the pretty hilltop village of **Grimaud**, capped by a ruined château.

La Citadelle et Musée Naval

The 16th-century fort is now a naval museum reflecting St-Tropez's maritime history.
Tel: 04 94 97 06 53. Open: Apr–Jun daily 10am–12.30pm & 1.30–6.30pm; Jul–Sept daily 10am–8pm; Oct–Mar daily 10am–12.30pm & 1.30–5.30pm. Admission charge.

Musée de l'Annonciade

This outstanding gallery contains the best selection of 1890–1950 paintings outside Paris: Braque, Dufy, Matisse and many others.
Place Grammont. Tel: 04 94 17 84 10. Open: winter Wed–Mon 10am–noon & 2–6pm; spring Wed–Mon 10am–1pm & 3–9pm; summer Wed–Mon 10am–1pm & 3–10pm. Closed: Nov. Admission charge.

St-Tropez is 68km (42½ miles) northeast of Toulon, off the N98.

Ste-Maxime

Ste-Maxime is an attractive, unpretentious resort. The seafront **Office de Tourisme** (*tel: 04 94 55 75 55. www.ste-maxime.com*) has a fascinating display of old postcards.

Musée des Traditions Locales

Items of local folklore and traditions are housed in a 16th-century tower.
Tour Carrée, place de l'Eglise. Tel: 04 94 96 70 30. Open: Wed–Sun 10am–noon & 3–6pm (till 7pm in Jul & Aug). Admission charge.

Ste-Maxime is across the bay from St-Tropez.

Toulon

Capital of the Var and France's second-largest naval base, Toulon is mainly a large and undistinguished city, with the exception of parts of the Vieille Ville (Old Town) behind quai

Stalingrad and quai de la Sinse, an area that escaped the bombings of World War II. North of the city, a cable car climbs to the summit of Mont Faron, from which you can appreciate Toulon's sheltered harbour.

Musée d'Art and the Musée d'Histoire Naturelle

These two museums, with the same address, present two quite different collections. The former contains an excellent collection of paintings and sculptures spanning some 500 years. The latter offers exhibits of stuffed birds, mammals, mineral and botanical items that put the area into perspective.
113 boulevard Leclerc.

Tel: 04 94 36 81 00.
Art Museum open: Tue–Sun noon–6pm.
Natural History Museum open: Mon–Fri 9am–6pm, Sat & Sun 11am–6pm.
Free admission to both.

Musée de la Marine

Toulon's long-standing associations with the sea are explained through model ships, drawings and memorabilia.
Place Monsenergue. Tel: 04 94 02 02 01.
www.musee-marine.fr.
Open: Jul & Aug daily 10am–6pm;
Sept–Jun Wed–Mon 10am–6pm.
Closed: Jan. Admission charge.

Toulon is 69km (43 miles) southwest of St-Tropez.

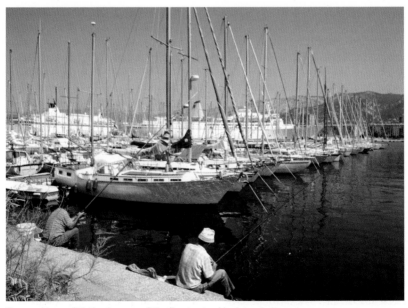

The naval base of Toulon has one of the finest natural harbours in France

Tour: L'Estérel

The Massif de l'Estérel, a mountain range which rises to 618m (2028ft), is the perfect antidote to the Côte d'Azur's overdevelopment. This wild, rugged and largely impenetrable upland, covered in maquis *(scrub), a dense covering of heathers, gorse, mimosa, lavender and other shrubs, has a coastal equivalent along the indented Corniche de l'Estérel.*

Allow a full day, including some time to stop off at the coast.

From Fréjus, take the coast road via the marina to St-Raphaël (see p81). On leaving St-Raphaël by the D1098 coast road you will soon be among the rich red volcanic rocks, small coves and sand-and-pebble beaches that characterise the Corniche de l'Estérel (its nickname is the Corniche d'Or, the 'Golden Corniche'). The Île d'Or, which lies in the bay off Plage du Dramont, was the inspiration for the cover of Tintin and the Black Island by Hergé. On the approach to Agay, you get to enjoy many excellent views of craggy, burnished mountains tumbling down into open seas.

1 Agay

Agay is the only resort of any significant size on the Corniche, and a refreshing change from the pseudo-sophistication of some of its better-known sister resorts. Its attractive beach and small harbour lie snugly protected within a sheltered horseshoe-shaped bay, surrounded by the Estérel Mountains.

From Agay you can take a detour inland, initially along the D100, and then turning right after a few kilometres along a twisting road through the hills for the superb viewpoints of the Pic du Cap Roux (452m/1,483ft), the Pic d'Aurelle (323m/1,060ft) and the Pic de l'Ours (496m/1,627ft).

The coast road from Agay leads to the smaller seaside centre of Anthéor and Anthéor-Plage (Beach). Le Trayas, just before Miramar, is the highest point on the Corniche. The road overlooks a rugged section of coastline, though there is an abrupt change of scene on the approach to Théoule-sur-Mer when Cannes and the densely developed Golfe de Napoule come into view. Carry on to La Napoule.

2 La Napoule

The small resort of La Napoule, with its large, boat-filled harbour, marks the start of the Riviera proper. Its château, dating from the 14th century, was much altered by American sculptor

Henry Clews at the start of the 20th century. Critics call it a tasteless folly. See if you agree by taking a guided tour (*tours available, Mar–Oct Wed–Mon afternoons; tel: 04 93 49 95 05; www.chateau-lanapoule.com*). *You can also visit by yourself (mid-Feb–Oct daily 10am–6pm; Nov–mid-Feb daily 2–5pm). For the return leg of the tour, follow the DN7 inland, a scenic road that skirts the northern slopes of the Massif de l'Estérel, following mainly the Roman route Via Aurelia. The Auberge des Adrets was the haunt of a highwayman in the 18th century. About 5km (3 miles) after the Auberge, turn left for Mont Vinaigre.*

3 Mont Vinaigre

Mont Vinaigre, at 618m (2,028ft), is the highest point in the Massif (there are also spectacular views from the Col de l'Aire de l'Olivier just to the south). This is excellent walking country, with a good network of trails and picnic areas. *Return to the DN7, a road that twists and turns on the descent to Fréjus.*

4 Chapelle Notre-Dame-de-Jérusalem

Stop off at this chapel. Its single chamber is brightly decorated with murals designed by Jean Cocteau. Further along the road, just a few kilometres from Fréjus, is a Vietnamese pagoda, used as a Buddhist temple.

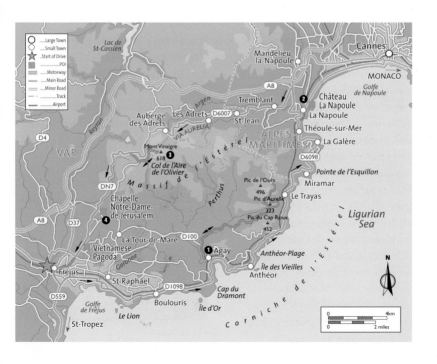

Alpes-Maritimes

The busiest stretch of the Côte d'Azur – including the tiny independent Principality of Monaco – lies between Cannes and the Italian border. This is the Riviera at its most incandescent and infuriating. The contrast between coast and country could not be more striking. Within an hour's drive of the Mediterranean is a département *of hidden valleys, remote, inaccessible uplands and wild Alpine scenery.*

Antibes

The Cap d'Antibes promontory jutting out into the Mediterranean between Cannes and Nice is made up of two fashionable resorts, Antibes and Juan-les-Pins (*see pp100–101*). Antibes, on the eastern shore, is a honeypot for celebrities and the seriously rich. The millionaires in search of more privacy hide themselves away in their exclusive mansions around Cap d'Antibes.

Antibes also attracts artists. Picasso's studio was at **Château Grimaldi**, an unmissable landmark on the headland above the old town. The medieval château and stout sea wall guard Antibes's characterful old quarter, far more enticing than the busy, bland modern town further inland. Look out among the narrow streets for the cathedral (noted for its magnificent early 18th-century doors) and unapologetically workaday covered market. The **Vieux Port** (Old Port) has been completely dwarfed by the massive modern harbour of

neighbouring **Port Vauban**, nickknamed 'billionaires' wharf' – mooring place of some of Europe's most fabulous yachts – overlooked by the 16th-century Fort Carré.

Musée d'Archéologie

Antibes has a long history. This museum tells the story of Etruscan, Greek, Roman and medieval settlement here. *Bastion St-André. Tel: 04 92 90 53 36. Open: mid-Jun–mid-Sept Tue–Sun 10am–noon & 2–6pm; mid-Sept–mid-*

Musée Picasso, Antibes

Alpes-Maritimes

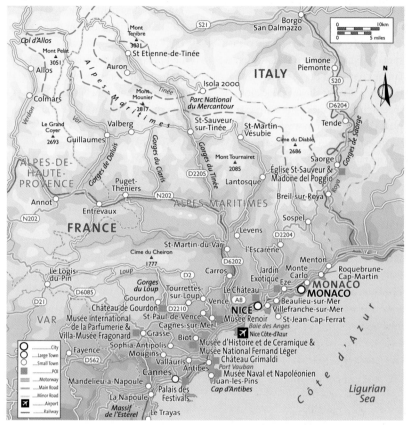

Jun Tue–Sun 10am–noon & 2–5pm. Admission charge.

Musée Picasso

Picasso worked 'like a madman' for the two months, from September to November 1946, he spent at Château Grimaldi, achieving new heights of creative genius. His gift to Antibes for the use of the château was the artistic output of his stay. This outstanding collection forms the basis of the Picasso Museum, later enriched by his tapestries, ceramics, engravings and lithographs. It also has paintings and sculptures from other leading artists such as Miró, de Staël, Léger and Ernst, and photographs of Picasso by Michel Sima and other friends.

Château Grimaldi, place Marijol. Tel: 04 92 90 54 20. Open: Jun–Sept Tue–Sun 10am–6pm; Oct–May Tue–Sun 10am–noon & 2–6pm. Antibes is 11km (7 miles) northeast of Cannes.

Beaulieu-sur-Mer and St-Jean-Cap-Ferrat

The small resort of Beaulieu is less stately than it once was, but it's still a stylish spot, with La Reserve, one of the most famous hotels on the coast, and some majestic villas. Its sheltered location means that it is one of the warmest places on the coast in winter. It also has a yacht marina with several restaurants, and a fine 19th-century casino.

The neighbouring peninsula of St-Jean-Cap-Ferrat is full of millionaires' villas and lush vegetation. It has a small harbour (St-Jean itself) with lively bars and restaurants, and several luxury hotels. There is a pleasant walk along the coast from St-Jean to Beaulieu, and a dramatic coastal footpath from Paloma beach to Pointe St-Hospice. The lighthouse at the southern tip of the cape has fine views.

Villa Ephrussi de Rothschild

A palatial villa complete with fascinating art and furniture. There are wonderful views from the stunning series of gardens.
1 avenue Ephrussi-de-Rothschild. Tel: 04 93 01 33 09. Open: Feb–Oct 10am–6pm; Jul & Aug till 7pm); Nov–Jan Mon–Fri 2–6pm, Sat–Sun 10am–6pm. Admission charge.

Villa Kérylos

Built in the early 1900s as a reproduction of an ancient Greek villa. Joint ticket with the Villa Ephrussi de Rothschild,

The narrow streets of medieval Biot are full of craft studios and shops

and the same opening times.
Impasse Gustave-Eiffel. Tel: 04 93 01 01 44. Admission charge.

Beaulieu is 15km (9½ miles) north of Aix-en-Provence, on the D14c.

Biot

The bond between Vallauris and Picasso (*see pp115 & 118*) is mirrored by Biot's strong links with Fernand Léger (1881–1955). The village was Léger's home for the last few years of his life, and is the location of an important museum dedicated to the artist.

The medieval village, well known for its pottery and glassware, is a mixture of gateways, narrow lanes and sloping streets. Most visitors make for the rue St-Sébastien, where the potteries and glass shops are concentrated. You can see glassblowers at work in the Verrerie de Biot on chemin des Combes; the shop is on rue St-Sébastien.

Musée d'Histoire et de Céramique

A restored kitchen is one of the exhibits in this museum of local life and ceramics.
9 rue Saint-Sébastien. Tel: 04 93 65 54 54. Open: summer Wed–Sun 10am–6pm; winter Wed–Sun 2–6pm. Admission charge.

Musée National Fernand Léger

A complete cross-section of the artist's work is on display at this museum, from early post-Cubism to the more direct man-and-industry canvases of his later period.

Off the D4 southeast of the village. Chemin du Val de Pome. Tel: 04 92 91 50 30. www.musee-fernandleger.fr. Open: Jun–Oct Wed–Mon 10am–6pm; Nov–May Wed–Mon 10am–5pm. Admission charge.

Biot is on the D4, accessible off the N7, in the hills north of Antibes.

Cagnes-sur-Mer

The best part of ungainly, sprawling Cagnes-sur-Mer is Haut-de-Cagnes, the old medieval quarter set high on a ridge overlooking the coast. Here, you will find the usual 'perched village' picture of perfection: an ancient château (now a museum-cum-art gallery), exquisite homes and expensive restaurants, on a wooded outcrop prettified by sweet-scented ornamental gardens.

Back along the coast, Cagnes is famous for its racecourse-by-the-sea and associations with Auguste Renoir.

Musée Renoir

Parts of the house in which Renoir spent the last 11 years of his life look as if the artist is still at work.
La Maison de Renoir, Les Collettes. Tel: 04 93 20 61 07. Open: May–Sept Wed–Mon 10am–noon & 2–6pm; Oct–Apr Wed–Mon 10am–noon & 2–5pm. Closed: early Dec. Admission charge.

Cagnes-sur-Mer is between Nice and Antibes.

Cannes

Cannes is big, busy and, amazingly enough, still beautiful in parts. In 1834 the English Lord Chancellor, Lord Brougham, arrived here after fleeing from cholera-stricken Nice. He liked what he saw, built a villa and – voilà! – the resort was born. Constant redevelopment continues apace on this febrile stretch of coast: the Cannes of today is not even a resort in the usual sense, more a year-round meeting place for businesspeople, conference delegates and, of course, film stars.

The hub of modern Cannes is the **Palais des Festivals**, the vast convention centre overlooking the **Vieux Port** (Old Port). This great lump of a building, opened in 1982, illustrates where the priorities of the town planners lie. Everything is laid on with maximum convenience for the delegates. The immaculately tended main beaches are to the right and left, while the seafront boulevard de la Croisette is but a stone's throw away (the Carlton hotel's sculpted, gleaming white façade really does look like a piece of wedding cake).

To return to reality, you have to climb the hill into **Le Suquet**, the old quarter on the western side of the port. Founded by the Romans, it later became the property of the monks of the **Îles de Lérins** a short distance offshore. Tour Le Suquet, the 11th-century watch tower crowning the summit, is a magnificent viewpoint. Also here is the Musée de la Castre and the Église Notre-Dame d'Espérance, completed in 1648.

If you are on a budget, then the restaurants in Le Suquet's narrow streets are your best bet for eating out. Back in the main town, rue d'Antibes and rue Meynadier are Cannes's fashionable shopping thoroughfares, though for more down-to-earth produce there is the covered market, the Marché Forville.

The quietest side of Cannes is at La Croisette at the end of the boulevard. But if you really want to get away from it all, then take the 20-minute boat trip from the Vieux Port to the tranquil islands known collectively as the Îles de

The old port of Cannes is less glitzy than the rest of town

Lérins: **St-Honorat**, with its monastic associations, and the larger **Ste-Marguerite**.

Mougins, a short distance inland from Cannes, is a delightful perched village of expensive restaurants and exclusive shops. It stands on a 260m (853ft) high outcrop, insulated from the busy world at its feet.

Musée de la Castre

Located in the old citadel, the museum contains antiquities from many countries and cultures – Mediterranean, Egyptian, Far Eastern, South American, etc. There is also a permanent exhibition of Provençal landscapes.
Place de la Castre, Le Suquet. Tel: 04 93 38 55 26. Open: Oct–Mar Tue–Sun 10am–1pm & 2–5pm; Apr–Jun & Sept 10am–1pm & 2–6pm; Jul & Aug Tue–Sun 10am–7pm. Admission charge.

Musée de la Mer (Museum of the Sea)

This museum is within the fort on the island of Ste-Marguerite. Not just maritime in theme, its exhibits include items from local shipwrecks, artefacts excavated on the island, and the rooms of the old state prison at the fort, including the cell of the fabled Man in the Iron Mask.
Fort Royal, Île Ste-Marguerite. Tel: 04 93 38 55 26. Open: Apr & May Tue–Sun 10.30am–1.15pm & 2.15–5.45pm; Jun–Sept daily 10am–5.45pm; Oct–Mar Tue–Sun 10.30am–1.15pm & 2.15–4.45pm. Admission charge.

SOPHIA-ANTIPOLIS

Driving between Nice and Cannes, you will see signs to Sophia-Antipolis, a vast science and technology park that forms part of the Côte d'Azur's plans for continuing economic success. Although it has yet to eclipse tourism in its revenues, it has proved a fine base for investment in the 'sun belt'.

Set up as a long-term experiment in the early 1970s by Pierre Lafitte, Sophia-Antipolis was conceived to be 'a city of science, culture and wisdom'. It took the Greek word for wisdom and paired it with the name for their ancient settlement at nearby Antibes. It is Europe's equivalent of California's Silicon Valley, and has, over the last three decades, morphed into a successful economic zone where the accent is now on R&D, telecommunications, IT, academia and other non-polluting industries. In total, some 1,100 companies have set up in Sophia-Antipolis employing over 21,000 staff. These include the big names France Telecom, IBM, Siemens, AT&T and Alcatel.

In the dog-eat-dog IT business of the last few years, many of the companies that originally moved here have been absorbed by others, but, significantly, few of the employees have considered relocating. Instead they have sought work within the Riviera area, or have set up their own firms.

Eze

Of all the perched villages inland from the coast, Eze is the most dramatic. It is precariously balanced on a jagged, precipitous outcrop. The easiest approach is along the N7 – you can, if you are lucky, find a space in the car park at the foot of the village and then walk up into the maze of narrow vaulted passageways, crooked steps and hidden corners. It is nowadays almost
(*Cont. on p98*)

Alpes-Maritimes

Cannes Film Festival

There is only one place for the world's film-makers to be in May – Cannes, home of the International Film Festival. For two weeks the resort swarms with producers, directors, stars, starlets, minders, has-beens, hangers-on, deal-makers, journalists, moguls and would-be moguls. Deals are struck by hotel pools or in expensive restaurants in an atmosphere as unreal as anything created on a Hollywood set.

Born of rivalry

Curiously, all this hype and hysteria

The Film Festival is held in the Palais des Festivals et des Congrès

would never have come about at all had it not been for Benito Mussolini. The Italian dictator inaugurated the Venice Film Festival in the mid-1930s. The French, in retaliation for the fact that all the major prizes went to Fascist-oriented films, devised a rival festival. Their timing was less than serendipitous: set for a launch in September 1939, the festival was postponed until 1946 owing to the outbreak of war.

The new festival was not an overnight success. But in the mid-1950s, Brigitte Bardot made a huge impact at Cannes, and by the end of the decade American influence – and money – transformed the festival into a frenetic event characterised by wheeling and dealing, unbridled excess and controlled chaos.

Coming of age

Cannes in the 1960s became Hollywood's shop window in Europe (Cannes is, after all, twinned with Beverly Hills), and as the TV industry expanded worldwide, followed by video, satellite and cable, the scale of the festival increased dramatically. The main site of the festival moved from its old location in the middle of Croisette

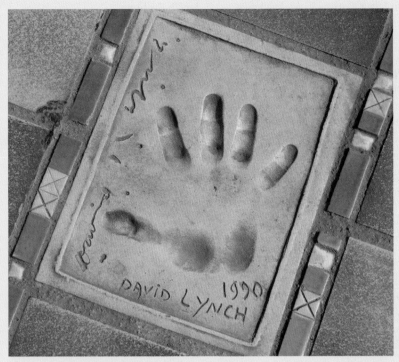

The handprint of American director David Lynch at Cannes

(where the Palais Stephanie hotel is today) to the vast, bunker-like Palais des Festivals in 1982. The building has two auditoriums, a theatre, and a huge, subterranean exhibition space, where much of the sales activity takes place. Today, about 50,000 people descend on Cannes each year, and hotel prices go up accordingly. The best film is awarded the Palme d'Or – the Golden Palm – by the Cannes jury, which is made up of respected figures from the film industry (including actors, directors and screenwriters); it is the highest accolade in film after the mighty Oscar.

You'll be lucky to glimpse a movie star, however, unless you gather round the Palais entrance before a screening, or hang around the Carlton, Martinez or Majestic hotels. In any case, the most famous actors tend to stay in villas, or luxury hotels further along the coast. And, although there are screenings you can attend at local cinemas, don't expect to be able to access official shows: entrance is by invitation only.

entirely a tourist village of galleries, restaurants and shops, yet they fail to eclipse Eze's breathtaking setting 470m (1,542ft) above sea level, and the integrity of its restored medieval architecture.

Paradoxically, its strongest point – the original castle – has suffered most from the ravages of time. Thankfully, the 14th-century Chapelle des Pénitents Blancs on place du Planet is in rather better condition. Its chief glory is an unusual Catalan crucifix of the mid-13th century that depicts a smiling Christ.

Jardin Exotique

This unusual garden of cacti and succulents is located among the ruins of Eze's castle.

Tel: 04 93 41 26 00. Open: summer daily 9am–8pm; winter daily 9am–dusk. Admission charge.

Eze is between Monaco and Nice.

Gourdon

Spectacularly located, Gourdon is another sheer-sided perched village. Although there are one or two classy shops selling perfume and soap, it is

The panorama from Eze's Jardin Exotique

best to ignore the tacky tourist knick-knacks and concentrate instead on the castle with its superb Le Nôtre-designed gardens and a magnificent view of the coast.

Château de Gourdon

The immaculately restored 13th-century castle has an excellent display of arms and armour, and an interesting art collection.
Tel: 04 93 09 68 02. Open: Jun–Sept daily 11am–1pm & 2–7pm; Oct–May Wed–Mon 2–6pm. Admission charge.

Gourdon is on the D3, 14km (9 miles) northeast of Grasse.

Grasse

This pleasant town, set in shallow but sheltering hill country less than 20km (12 miles) from the coast, has a graceful, calming air. Its surrounding meadowlands yield the fragrant flowers that have made Grasse famous as a perfume town. Whenever you visit you will be assailed by fragrance: mimosas in spring, roses and lavender in summer, jasmine in autumn. The town has not been able to distance itself completely from the overdevelopment along the coast. But although Grasse has its modern housing and high-technology parks, it is still an appealing mixture of the handsome and the humble: fine old buildings and traditional workaday shopping streets.

These two contrasting sides to Grasse are closest together along the elegant

Sundial in Gourdon

terraced gardens in front of the grand **Palais des Congrès**. Take the steps down into rue Jean-Ossola and you are immediately enclosed within an old town of narrow streets. A daily market is held at place aux Aires, while place du Petit-Puy is the site of Grasse's cathedral, dating from the 12th century. It is well worth devoting some time to this part of Grasse and its museums, despite the town's overwhelming association with perfume (*see box p100*). There are some 30 *parfumeries* in and around the town (ask for details at the **Office de Tourisme**, Palais des Congrès, *tel: 04 93 36 66 66*).

Musée International de la Parfumerie

Reopened after extensive refurbishment in 2008, this museum deals with the history and manufacture of perfume.
8 place du Cours. Tel: 04 97 05 58 00. Open: Jun–Sept daily 10am–7pm; Oct & Dec–May Wed–Sun 11am–6pm. Closed: Nov. Admission charge.

PERFUME

The town of Grasse makes its living by bottling the scents of southern France.

Grasse's perfume industry began in the 16th century when immigrant Italian glovemakers decided to scent their leather gloves with perfume made from the local flowers. Today, around 30 major *parfumeries* are based in and around the town, using a mixture of imported and local materials to make perfumes, many of which are sold under brand names such as Dior and Estée Lauder. Huge quantities of floral material go into the creation of the highly concentrated essences known as essential oils or absolutes. The art of the perfumer lies in the blending of these and other ingredients.

Many of Grasse's *parfumeries* welcome visitors, and there are museums in the town that explain the history and manufacture of perfume.

Villa-Musée Fragonard

Works by Fragonard can be seen in this 18th-century villa in which the artist lived. Not to be confused with the Parfumerie Fragonard, at 20 boulevard Fragonard, which is a perfume factory and museum with guided tours (free admission).

23 boulevard Fragonard.
Tel: 04 97 05 58 00. Open: Jun–Sept daily 10am–6.30pm; Oct & Dec–May Wed–Sun 10am–12.30pm & 2–5.30pm. Closed: Nov. Admission charge. Grasse is 20km (12 miles) northwest of Cannes.

Isola 2000

This is one for the skiing enthusiasts. Despite the fact that it is one of the southernmost Alpine resorts and only 1½ hours from Nice, Isola has a good snow record. If you are familiar with other French Alpine resorts, then Isola will hold no surprises. The functional approach, devoid of any Alpine charm, does at least deliver super-convenient doorstep skiing. Its unimaginative name derives from its altitude.

The resort, accessible by the tortuous D2205 through the Gorges of the Tinée, is only a few kilometres from the Italian border. Its proximity to the Parc National du Mercantour (*see pp137–8*) gives some credence to its claim of being a year-round resort, especially since accommodation costs are much lower in the summer 'off season'.

Further along the Tinée Valley is **Auron**, the oldest ski resort in the Alpes-Maritimes.

Juan-les-Pins

Juan-les-Pins is the place to be seen at night on the exclusive peninsula of Cap d'Antibes (*see also p90*). By day, you wonder what all the fuss is about, for Juan-les-Pins is an unexceptional little resort, neat and tidy but disappointingly bland. It wakes up after the sun goes down, when the clubs, bars and restaurants attract the Cap's well-heeled villa owners and glamour-seekers. F Scott Fitzgerald, aided and abetted by a few rich fellow Americans, colonised this stretch of coast in the 1920s, creating the fabulous myth that

Juan-les-Pins has been living off ever since. Part of Fitzgerald's novel *Tender Is the Night* is set here, and he wrote to a friend, 'I'd like to live and die on the French Riviera.' The town's jazz festival, the oldest of its kind in Europe, has become a major event since its founding in 1960.

Musée Naval et Napoléonien

Model ships, along with items relating to Napoleon's return from exile on Elba, and other memorabilia.
Batterie du Grillon, boulevard John-F-Kennedy (at Cap d'Antibes south of Juan-les-Pins).
Tel: 04 93 61 45 32.
Open: winter Tue–Sat 10am–4.30pm; summer Tue–Sat 10am–6pm. Admission charge.

Juan-les-Pins is a few kilometres from Antibes, on the opposite side of the Cap d'Antibes peninsula.

Menton

'Ma ville est un jardin' ('My town is a garden') claims the tourist literature for Menton – and for once it is right. Menton, almost within shouting distance of the Italian border, is the French Riviera's floral town par excellence. Its exceptional sunshine record, coupled with a subtropical climate and a patently garden-mad town council, have conspired to

Fragonard factory, Grasse

produce a resort bursting with colourful floral beds, luscious orange, lemon and palm trees, and beautiful award-winning areas of greenery. Where else would you find a place that holds a *Fête du Citron* in February, a festival of floats and tableaux made entirely of flowers, oranges and, of course, lemons?

Menton, unlike its more illustrious neighbours, has not embraced the growth-at-any-cost philosophy. Consequently, it is still a true resort as opposed to a conurbation by the sea. The **Vieille Ville** (Old Town), a cluster of pastel-shaded houses riddled with steep alleyways, has an almost Italianate air. All passageways eventually lead to place de la Conception on the highest ground above the **Vieux Port** (Old Port) and two ornate religious sites – the **Église de la Conception** and the **Église St-Michel**.

The sturdy fortified building on quai Napoléon pays homage to Jean Cocteau, though fans of the artist will also want to see the way he transformed the humble Salle des Mariages (registry office) in the Hôtel de Ville (Town Hall) in 1957.

West of quai Napoléon along baie du Soleil lies Menton's main beach. The promenade – and, for that matter, the entire resort – has an unexpectedly genteel, relaxed air, due in no small part to its popularity with elderly retired folk attracted by Menton's calm, sunny climate. The lucky ones are able to afford the villas in the hilly **Garavan** district

east of the Vieux Port, a gorgeous garden suburb thick with exotic vegetation and blessed with marvellous sea views. Avenue Katherine-Mansfield, named after the writer who had a retreat here, winds its way through this privileged quarter. Here you will also find the **Jardin des Colombières**, the best in the Garavan district and one of the finest on the Riviera.

Jardin du Val Rahmeh

Many species of both tropical and subtropical plants thrive in this botanical garden of the National Museum of Natural History.
Avenue Saint Jacques. Tel: 04 93 35 86 72. Open: May–Sept daily 10am–12.30pm & 3–6pm; Oct–Apr daily 10am–12.30pm & 2–5pm. Admission charge.

Musée Jean-Cocteau

Cocteau's paintings are beautifully presented in this 17th-century bastion. The painter and poet, who lived locally, designed the mosaic floor and donated many works of art.
Bastion du Vieux Port, quai Napoléon III. Tel: 04 93 57 72 30. Open: Wed–Mon 10am–noon & 2–6pm. Admission charge (free admission on first Sun of the month).
To see more of Cocteau's work visit the Chapelle Notre-Dame-de-Jérusalem near Fréjus (see p89).

Musée de la Préhistoire Régionale

The star attraction at this museum is the famous 'Menton Man', a 30,000-

year-old skull. Local traditions and culture are also covered.

Rue Lorédan-Larchey.
Tel: 04 93 35 84 64. Open: as for Musée Jean-Cocteau. Free admission.

Place de la Conception

The dominant building here is the Baroque **Église St-Michel**, pink and ochre outside and ornate within. The sunken square just outside is the venue for an atmospheric summer festival of chamber music. Close by is the **Église de la Conception**, built for the White Penitents in 1685. Restored in the 1980s, it has a wonderfully exuberant – or over-the-top, depending on taste – Baroque interior. (A third religious site, for the Black Penitents – the **Chapelle des Pénitents-Noirs** – stands a short distance away at the bottom of rue de Bréa.) The best

way to see the square is at night, during the famous summer chamber music festival.

Salle des Mariages

Cocteau's swirling, extravagant murals succeed admirably in his aim to 'create a theatrical setting . . . to offset the officialdom of a civil ceremony'.
Hôtel de Ville, place Ardoiono, rue de la République. Tel: 04 92 10 50 00.
Open: Mon–Fri 8.30am–12.30pm & 1.30–5pm. Admission charge.

Monaco

Even for those used to the tightly packed Riviera, Monaco comes as something of a shock. Not one square millimetre is wasted. High-rise buildings are crammed in, making the most of the limited space available in

(*Cont. on p106*)

Menton has been popular since the 19th century

Literary Provence

The literary tradition in Provence reaches all the way back to the troubadours, whose poems of courtly love encapsulate the most romantic aspect of medievalism. They were written in the Provençal language, which enjoyed a revival in the 19th century under the influence of poet Frédéric Mistral, who was awarded the Nobel Prize for Literature in 1904.

Marcel Pagnol (1895–1974) from Aubagne was a writer of novels, poems and short stories. His vision of Provence was captured in the atmospheric stories that became the award-winning films *Jean de Florette*

The landscape around Manosque inspired Jean Giono

and *Manon des Sources*. Jean Giono (1895–1970) was similarly inspired by the landscapes and the people of Provence – in his case, the area around his birthplace, Manosque.

The perfect workplace

Provence has arguably cast an even deeper spell over outsiders beguiled by its promise of sunshine and sensuality. In comparison to the bucolic works of its resident writers, literature of another kind was being written on the Riviera by leading American writers like F Scott Fitzgerald and Ernest Hemingway after World War I. In an era of prohibition and puritanism, they fled from what they regarded as the cultural wasteland of America to enjoy an easier lifestyle in the sun. Fitzgerald gave an evocative portrait of life in Cap d'Antibes in the 1920s in *Tender Is the Night*, but the idyll was bruised by his wife Zelda's affair with a young French aviator.

A writers' colony

Hemingway and his wife Hadley lived in a threesome on the Riviera with the American heiress Pauline Pfeiffer before moving on. In 1930 Aldous Huxley joined a writers' colony in the South of France, his neighbours including Thomas Mann and

Aldous Huxley was one of many foreign residents in the region

Cyril Connolly. The English novelist Somerset Maugham bought a house in Cap Ferrat in 1926 and spent at least six months every year there until his death in 1965, entertaining such celebrities as the Aga Khan, Winston Churchill, Noël Coward and Jean Cocteau.

An earlier arrival on the Riviera was the New Zealand-born British writer Katherine Mansfield, who died tragically young from TB. On a happier note, the 18-year-old Françoise Sagan achieved fame in the 1950s with her novel *Bonjour Tristesse*, a sharply defined love story set in a villa near Cannes. Other writers closely linked with the Riviera include Graham Greene and Anthony Burgess.

this 3km (2-mile) long tax haven. Historically a Greek, then a Roman colony, Monaco was bought from the Genoese by the Grimaldis. In 1346 the Grimaldi Charles I started building a fortress on the rocks of Monaco. Despite battles with the French crown resulting in the reduction of the principality, the Grimaldi dynasty has ruled over what has proved to be the world's longest-lasting democracy headed by a monarch.

Money is Monaco's *raison d'être*. The main casino is the most overt manifestation of the wealth that underpins this home of millionaires who, perfectly legally, avoid paying any income tax. And their wealth is protected in more ways than one. Monaco has more police officers per square kilometre than any other place in the world.

You might think that Monaco's artificiality, overindulgence and self-satisfaction make for a pretty rich diet – and you would be correct. But you should at least sample a little of it. There are compensations: the principality's immaculate, litter-free streets, its beautifully manicured gardens, and the undeniable spectacle of one of the world's most glamorous harbours full of some of the world's most expensive ocean-going palaces.

The densely populated principality is divided into a number of districts. Most visitor interest is concentrated in **Monaco-Ville**, the promontory west of the harbour (which contains the majority of the historic sites) and glitzy

Monte Carlo (the casino, conference and hotel district) to the east. Thanks to the many sporting, artistic and business events held there, Monaco has become a year-round destination.

La Collection de Voitures Anciennes (Historic Car Collection)

The late Prince Rainier's personal collection of over 100 classic cars. *Les Terraces de Fontvieille. Tel: (377) 92 05 28 56. Open: daily (except Christmas Day) 10am–6pm. Admission charge.*

Jardin Animalier

Tropical flora and fauna flourish in these gardens. *Terrasses de Fontvieille. Tel: (377) 93 50 40 30. Open: Jun–Sept daily 9am–noon & 2–7pm; Oct–Feb daily 10am–noon & 2–5pm Mar–May daily 10am–noon & 2–6pm. Admission charge.*

Jardin Exotique

Thousands of different exotic plants – including giant cacti – grow among rocks in this beautiful garden. You can also visit a cave with spectacular stalagmite and stalactite formations, and a museum of prehistory. *Boulevard du Jardin Exotique. Tel: (377) 93 15 29 80. Open: May–Sept daily 9am–7pm; Oct–Apr 9am–dusk. Admission charge.*

Musée Océanographique

Housed in a stunning neoclassical building poised over the cliff face, this museum of marine sciences contains the usual maritime specimens plus a famous 90-tank aquarium.

Avenue Saint-Martin.
Tel: (377) 93 15 36 00. www.oceano.mc.
Open: Apr–Jun & Sept daily
9.30am–7pm; Jul & Aug daily
9.30am–7.30pm; Oct–Mar daily
10am–6pm. Admission charge.

Palais Princier (Prince's Palace)

Outstanding features include the Italian-style gallery, the blue-and-gold Louis XV Salon and the Throne Room. The palace's South Wing contains a

The Palais Princier of Monaco

museum of Napoleonic souvenirs and historic archives.

Place du Palais. Tel: (377) 93 25 18 31.
Open: Jun–Sept daily 9.30am–6pm;
Oct daily 10am–5pm.
Closed: Nov–May. Call for museum
opening times. Admission charge.

Vieux Monaco

This historic part of Monaco has a number of interesting buildings in its narrow streets and alleys. Among these are the Palais de Justice, the fountain in place St-Nicolas, the placette Bosio, the Chapelle de la Paix, and the long brick Rampe Major linking La Condamine and the place du Palais.

Monaco is 21km (13 miles) east of Nice, off the A8/A805.

Nice

This noisy, seductive, teeming, vibrant city-by-the-sea takes some getting used to. You do not come to Nice for a quiet time; you come because of Nice's exhaustive stock of first-class museums; to sample its bubbling nightlife; to take a stroll down the famous promenade des Anglais; and for business, since Nice is the nucleus of a dynamic southern economy dubbed the 'California of Europe'. You might even spend time on the beach.

Nice is France's fifth-largest city – though it appears larger than it is as it cloaks its wooded hills, spreads behind into the fertile coastal plain and inches
(*Cont. on p110*)

Walk: Monaco

This walk concentrates on Monaco-Ville, the rocky promontory above the harbour dominated by the Palais Princier (Prince's Palace). In comparison to the hustle and bustle of the port below and the shops and casinos of Monte Carlo to the east, this part of the principality – the picturesque Old Town, a mixture of narrow streets, open spaces and gardens – seems positively sedate.

The walk can be comfortably completed in half a day.

From La Racasse hairpin (a name familiar to fans of Formula One Grand Prix racing) in La Condamine district, walk along quai Antoine 1er, taking a short detour left to the mouth of the port. Return to the yacht club on the quay, then climb the steps up towards the tubby-looking Fort Antoine, continuing

Monaco

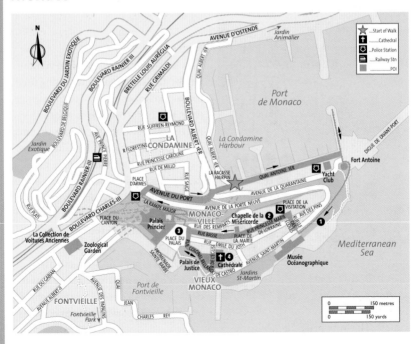

the climb into the gardens (signposted Palais, Musée).

1 Quay walk and gardens

The quieter side of the harbour leads to restful, shady gardens rising above Fort Antoine, an 18th-century defensive fortification now used as an outdoor theatre (*tel: (377) 93 15 80 00*).
Walk through the gardens to the Musée Océanographique, then take the pedestrianised street opposite – ruelle des Écoles – for place de la Visitation, turning left here for rue Princesse Marie de Lorraine.

2 Rue Princesse Marie de Lorraine

This cobbled street leads to the heart of the Old Town. The **Chapelle de la Miséricorde**, built 1639–45, was the seat of the Brotherhood of the Black Penitents, and contains a remarkable figure of Christ carved in wood.
Continue down rue Basse, a very narrow street lined with shops and cafés, which becomes even narrower before opening out into the huge open square, place du Palais.

3 Place du Palais

Place du Palais fronts the Palais Princier, the home of the Monégasque royal family, a mainly 19th-century building castellated for decorative effect only. The Changing of the Guard takes place here at 11.55am every day, a ceremony performed in full dress uniform (white in summer, black in winter). The lofty place du Palais is a

natural vantage point. Lined with cannons cast in the reign of Louis XIV, it looks down directly into the harbour, across to high-rise Monte Carlo and along the coast as far east as the Cape of Bordighera in Italy.
Leave place du Palais by rue Colonel Bellando de Castro, which brings you to the Palais de Justice and cathedral.

4 Cathédrale

The 19th-century cathedral, built in Romanesque-Byzantine style on the site of a 13th-century church dedicated to St Nicholas, contains tombs of former princes of Monaco. An episcopal throne in white marble and early 16th-century reredos are among its noteworthy features, though the cathedral's most-visited shrine is the tomb of Princess Grace (*open: daily 8.30am–7pm, until 6pm in winter*).
Return to place du Palais and descend this rocky outcrop by La Rampe Major, a staircase in the side of the cliff. Cross avenue de la Porte Neuve and follow avenue du Port back to the harbourside.

Monaco's cathedral contains the tomb of the much-loved Princess Grace

its way north and south along the shoreline. It enjoys a fine climate as it is largely protected from the bone-chilling *mistral* but is cooled by breezes from the deep blue Mediterranean Baie des Anges (Bay of Angels) during summer. A port, a resort and an ever-growing city, it has vastly improved its face in the last decade and is once again enjoying popularity with visitors. It is a wonderful city to discover and an excellent base from which to explore the allure of the Côte d'Azur and its magnificent hinterland.

It was the Romans who founded Cemenelum (now the Cimiez district), but the English, French and Italians have all had a hand in creating the Nice of today. English aristocrats gave the benevolent climate their stamp of approval. Italian nobility ruled here until 1860, when they handed the city over to the French and Nizza became Nice.

This mixed bag of influences is most apparent in the central area, where you will find the convincingly Italianate place Masséna (which really should be across the border!), the medieval **Vieille Ville**, the *belle époque* architecture, the extravagantly spacious gardens, the animated daily market along cours Saleya, and the main shopping streets. The one viewpoint from which it all starts to make sense is the 92m (302ft) high **Le Château**, not a castle but a wooded park. Beyond the shoreline, and up in the hills, are a number of lavish villas such as those in the Mont-

Boron and Cimiez districts – many still privately owned – that were constructed during the *belle époque* and fashionable 1950s. For the visitor with time, they are also worth looking at.

The only way to begin to get to know Nice is on foot. Many places of interest are within reasonable walking distance of the strip of coast that runs for a kilometre or so from Le Château hill along the promenade des Anglais. For the less energetic, a *petit train* (tourist train departing daily from the tourist office by the Jardins Albert 1er) plies the most popular tourist routes and helps you get your bearings – you can always go back by foot later.

The new tram system (inaugurated in late 2007) is a quick way of getting around the city centre.

Note that admission has been free to Nice's municipal museums since mid-2008.

The Riviera Pass (*www.niceriviera pass.com*) allows access to the museums that charge for admission in Nice, and to several other museums and attractions along the coast.

Other places to visit include the Villa Arson (contemporary modern art exhibits), Musée Terra Amata (a prehistoric collection and reconstruction of a 400,000-year-old campsite), the Baroque Cathédrale de Ste-Réparate and its square, Jardin Botanique (a fine collection of plants and trees, located in the western part of Nice), Palais de Justice, Opéra and the vibrant morning market in cours

Saleya. Further afield, the exclusive St-Jean-Cap-Ferrat and Villefranche are definitely worth visiting for their views, fine ports and numerous wealthy homes (some still inhabited by royalty), all discreetly veiled by lush palms and imposing walls.

Cathédrale Orthodoxe Russe de Saint Nicolas

An anomaly – but a glitteringly beautiful one – on the Nice horizon built in 1912 by the Tsarina Maria Feoderovna in memory of her son, the Grand Duke Nicholas. It was the first, and remains the finest, Russian church outside Russia.

Avenue Nicholas II. Tel: 04 93 96 88 02. Open: Jun–Sept daily 9am–noon & 2–6pm; Oct–May daily 9.30am–noon & 2.30–5.30pm. Closed for Mass 10am–noon Sun, and Orthodox holidays. Admission charge.

Hôtel Negresco

Nice's most famous landmark, this exotic *belle époque* hotel was built for the Romanian Henri Negresco in 1912 by Belgian architect Edouard Niermans. It has hosted among others Queen Elizabeth II, Emperor Hirohito, Churchill, Rockefeller, the Beatles, Picasso, Charlie Chaplin, Marlon Brando and Frank Sinatra. Still the city's most exclusive hotel, it enjoys immense popularity for its historic past, contemporary luxury and prime position on the promenade.
*37 promenade des Anglais.
Tel: 04 93 16 64 00.*

Musée d'Archéologie

Exhibits span the Bronze Age down to the Middle Ages. It stands on the edge of excavated 3rd-century Roman baths with 5th-century religious buildings and offers a number of

The busy old port of Nice

archaeological items found on this Roman site. Take time afterwards to explore the garden of the amphitheatre of Cimiez. This is the site of Nice's annual Jazz Festival.

160 avenue des Arènes de Cimiez. Tel: 04 93 81 59 57. Open: Wed–Mon 10am–6pm. Free admission.

Musée d'Art Moderne et d'Art Contemporain

A permanent collection consisting mainly of neo-Realism and Pop Art – definitely for aficionados of modern art. There is a great view of Old Nice from the rooftop.

Promenade des Arts. Tel: 04 97 13 42 01. Open: Tue–Sun 10am–6pm. Free admission.

Musée des Arts Asiatiques

Gleaming white marble in this Kenzo Tange-designed museum provides the backdrop for this collection of classical and contemporary works from different regions of Asia. The museum is located on an island in an artificial lake in the midst of a 7-hectare (17-acre) garden.

405 promenade des Anglais. Tel: 04 92 29 37 00. www.arts-asiatiques.com. Open: summer Wed–Mon 10am–6pm; winter Wed–Mon 10am–5pm. Free admission.

Musée des Beaux-Arts (Museum of Fine Arts)

The gallery has a large collection of 17th- to 19th-century paintings plus sculptures, and also hosts temporary art exhibits. Once the private home of

Ukrainian Princess Kotschoubey, the elegant mansion also has pleasant shady gardens.

33 avenue des Baumettes. Tel: 04 92 15 28 28. Open: Tue–Sun 10am–6pm. Free admission.

Musée Franciscain et Monastère de Cimiez

Devoted to the life and work of the Franciscan monks, the museum includes three Gothic paintings by renowned local artist Louis Bréa. The beautiful flower-filled gardens are also open to the public.

Place du Monastère. Tel: 04 93 81 00 04. Open: Mon–Sat 10am–noon & 3–6pm. Free admission.

Musée d'Histoire Naturelle

Over a million objects fill this large museum, which is a treasure trove for the young.

Museum of Fine Arts, Nice

60 bis boulevard Risso. Tel: 04 97 13 46
80. Open: Tue–Sun 10am–6pm.
Free admission.

Musée International d'Art Naïf Anatoly Jakovsky

A fine collection of naïve art from the
last two centuries acquired from all
over the world. Located in the former
home of the perfumer François Coty.
Château Sainte-Helene, avenue de
Fabron. Tel: 04 93 71 78 33. Open:
Wed–Mon 10am–6pm. Free admission.

Musée Matisse

Matisse settled in Nice in 1917 and
died here in 1954. His personal
collection is displayed in a splendid
17th-century villa in Cimiez, Nice's
smart suburb.
164 avenue des Arènes de Cimiez.
Tel: 04 93 81 08 08. www.musee-matisse-
nice.org. Open: Wed–Mon 10am–6pm.
Free admission.

Musée National Marc Chagall

This is the place for lovers of the
colourful work of Russian émigré
Chagall. His fabulist style is given full
expression in a series of paintings, a
'Biblical Message' based on the Old
Testament. But many of his other works
– paintings, stained glass, gouaches,
drawings and mosaics – are also well
displayed in this important museum.
Avenue du Docteur-Ménard.
Tel: 04 93 53 87 20. Open: summer
Wed–Mon 10am–6pm; winter Wed–Mon
10am–5pm. Admission charge.

Palais Lascaris

Decorative arts dating from the Baroque
period and state rooms decorated with
17th- and 18th-century frescoes make
this one of the more impressive places
to visit. The palace is noted for its
Baroque staircase. It also contains a
reconstructed 18th-century pharmacy.
15 rue Droite. Tel: 04 93 62 72 40.
Open: Wed–Mon 10am–6pm.
Free admission.

Nice is about 200km (125 miles)
northeast of Marseille, off the A8.

St-Paul-de-Vence

Some perched villages are famous for
their restaurants, others for their real
estate. St-Paul is famous for its art.
Galleries are everywhere. The village
has made a lot of concessions to
tourists: few of the medieval houses
along its main street seem to serve their
original purpose, having been
converted into expensive galleries and
bright T-shirt and souvenir shops. Its
arty associations reach their zenith at
the Fondation Maeght. The village even
displays its cultural pretensions on its
pavements, which are decorated with
pebbles arranged in artistic swirls and
patterns. Nevertheless, St-Paul has a
distinctive charm.

The main gate into the village is
alongside the Café de la Place, a lovely
old-fashioned café complete with boules
pitch outside. Just by the pitch is the
Colombe d'Or hotel, famous for its
magnificent collection of modern art.

These pieces were donated by some of the greatest names of the 20th century in exchange for food and lodging. St-Paul's unbroken ring of 16th-century walls protects a medieval village dominated by a hilltop church. The 12th-century Église de St-Paul-de-Vence has a tall 18th-century bell tower that is almost matched in height by the giant palm tree growing beside it.

Fondation Maeght

Created in the 1960s by collectors Aimé and Marguerite Maeght, this unique purpose-built arts centre eschews the established concepts of entrance, exit and the *sens de la visite*. Nothing is arranged conventionally. Outside, you will encounter modern sculpture set tongue-in-cheek against water, trees and stone walls. Permanent and temporary exhibitions are held in the centre's airy split-level galleries. It is near the approach to the village.
Montée des Trious. Tel: 04 93 32 81 63.

www.fondation-maeght.com.
Open: Jul–Sept daily 10am–7pm; Oct–Jun daily 10am–12.30pm & 2.30–6pm. Admission charge.

Musée d'Histoire Locale

The most important events in the lives of the people of St-Paul are reflected in the museum's tableaux and exhibits.
Place de l'Eglise. Tel: 04 93 32 41 13. Open: Apr–Oct daily 10am–noon & 3–6pm; Dec–Mar daily 2–5pm. Closed: Nov. Admission charge.

St-Paul-de-Vence is in the hills between Nice and Antibes.

Saorge

High in the Alpes-Maritimes close to the Italian border, this village is accessible by the N204 through the Gorges de Saorge, a dramatic defile carved by the tumbling River Roya. The fortified village was built to control communications into the high country

Saorge, a 'stacked village' dramatically perched on the mountainside

of the Haute Roya, a hybrid area of Italian and French influences which only became French territory in 1947.

Saorge, its terraces piled haphazardly one above the other on a savage slope, is a spectacular sight. This *village empilé* (stacked village) is the mountain equivalent of the perched villages along the coast. Its impossibly steep cobbled alleyways and confusing tiers of streets eventually lead up to the 15th-century Église St-Sauveur and a Franciscan monastery. Further up still is the isolated 11th-century Romanesque chapel of Madone del Poggio.

Higher up the valley, close to the border, is the unequivocally Italianate village of **Tende**, while to the south lies restful **Breil-sur-Roya**, centre of the local olive oil industry (*see pp160–61*). *Saorge is close to the Italian border, 47km (29 miles) north of Menton.*

Tourrettes-sur-Loup

This picturesque village is partly misnamed. Its medieval towers (*tours*) are evident enough, but the River Loup is elsewhere, in the rolling, wooded hills to the south. The village's Grand-Rue is also misleadingly named: narrow, crooked and atmospheric, it winds its way past ancient, rough-stoned houses, some of which have been converted into potteries, craft workshops and galleries, while others still await restoration.

From Tourrettes, take the D2210 to Pont-du-Loup, turning northwards along the D6 for the craggy **Gorges du Loup**. The narrow road, chiselled out of the rock face, wriggles up a steep-sided valley beside the foaming river. At the top end of the gorge, return south on the D3, which climbs to give wonderful views down into the vertical-sided valley. *Tourrettes-sur-Loup is about 22km (14 miles) northeast of Grasse.*

Vallauris

If you do not like pottery, then give Vallauris a miss. The town's love affair with pots is flaunted quite unselfconsciously. Oversized urns, serving as giant flowerpots, line the smart shopping streets in the modern town beneath the old quarter of the Vieille Ville (Old Town) with its Renaissance château.

Vallauris's pottery pedigree dates back to Roman times. By the end of World War II, the industry was on its last legs. Revival came when Pablo Picasso took an interest, spending two prolific years at the Madoura pottery workshop in the town. Other artists followed in his wake. Vallauris was back in the pottery business.

Most of the potteries are located along the main street, avenue Georges-Clemenceau; the Madoura pottery, which still sells Picasso designs, is off the main street along avenue des Anciens Combattants d'AFN. In the place de la Libération, the town's main square and marketplace, is the life-size bronze statue *Man Holding a Sheep*, Picasso's gift to the town in 1950.

(*Cont. on p118*)

Art in Provence

The vivid colours and intense light of the South of France have enticed many artists to Provence, including – in recent centuries – Van Gogh (*see pp56–7*), Monet and Renoir in the 19th century, and Matisse and Picasso in the 20th.

19th century

Claude Monet first visited the region in 1883 and returned in 1888 to stay in Antibes and Juan-les-Pins. He followed the custom of the age by spending winter and early spring in the south and shrewdly painted

Cézanne's studio: a still life in itself

local beauty spots in order to attract collectors.

Auguste Renoir spent the winter of 1889–90 in the south and settled in Cagnes-sur-Mer in 1905. Crippled by rheumatoid arthritis, he continued to paint with a brush wedged between his rigid fingers, completing more than 6,000 pictures in his lifetime.

Paul Cézanne was a home-grown talent. He spent much of his life in his birthplace, Aix-en-Provence (where he died in 1906), gradually establishing a reputation which today places him as a master of Post-Impressionism and one of the forerunners of modern art.

The subject of Van Gogh's *Café Terrace at Night* (1888) still exists

20th century

Henri Matisse and Raoul Dufy were among the *fauves* ('wild beasts'), so-called because of their aggressive use of strong colour, who also followed the Impressionists. The most influential artist of the 20th century, Pablo Picasso, often spent his summers at Juan-les-Pins between the wars, and in 1946 he left Paris for good to settle on the Riviera. The lifestyle had a liberating effect, and even in extreme old age he created 1,000 works of art in five years. A lifetime of creativity ended in April 1973, when he died at the age of 92.

The success of Picasso and Matisse offended another great artist associated with the Riviera, Marc Chagall. He settled there to show the world he was their equal, moving to St-Jean-Cap-Ferrat in 1949. In the 1950s Nice produced the school of artists known as Nouveaux Realistes, who reacted against figurative art and abstract painting. One of its exponents, Yves Klein, coated the bodies of nude models with paint and ordered them to crawl over the canvases. Whatever would Van Gogh have made of that?

Musée de la Céramique Kitsch

An amusing collection celebrating some of the more bizarre offerings on sale to tourists over the years.

Rue de la Fontaine. Tel: 04 93 64 71 83. Open: Sept–Jun Wed–Mon 10am–12.15pm & 2–5pm (till 6pm late Jun and early Sept); Jul & Aug daily 10am–7pm. Admission charge.

Musée Magnelli

Housed in the château, the museum contains an excellent collection of ceramics – including pieces by Picasso – and paintings by Italian artist Alberto Magnelli (1888–1971).

Place de la Libération. Tel: 04 93 64 71 83. Open: Sept–Jun Wed–Mon 10am–12.15pm & 2–5pm (till 6pm late Jun and early Sept); Jul & Aug daily 10am–7pm. Admission charge.

Musée National Picasso

In 1952 Picasso decorated the walls of Vallauris's 13th-century Romanesque chapel (in the château's courtyard) with a huge War and Peace tableau.

Place de la Libération. Tel: 04 93 64 71 83. www.musee-picasso-vallauris.fr. Open: Sept–Jun Wed–Mon 10am–12.15pm & 2–5pm (till 6pm late Jun and early Sept); Jul & Aug daily 10am–7pm. Admission charge.

Vallauris is 7.5km (4¾ miles) west of Antibes on the D135.

Vence

After its high-flying neighbour, St-Paul-de-Vence (*see pp113–14*), Vence brings you back down to earth. The thousands who have moved here in recent decades, attracted by the gentle climate and the booming Sun Belt industries, have created something of an urban sprawl around the old town. But they have also brought a vitality and renewed purpose to Vence, without damaging the inherent charm of its historic centre.

Vallauris is famous for its pottery

Colourful church façade in Vence

white murals – a surprise to many – finds a counterpoint in his marvellous stained-glass windows.

466 avenue Henri-Matisse. Tel: 04 93 58 03 26. Open: Mon, Wed & Sat 2–5.30pm; Tue & Thur 10–11.30am & 2–5.30pm. Other times by prior arrangement. Closed: Nov. Admission charge.

Vence is 24km (15 miles) west of Nice.

Villefranche-sur-Mer

Founded in the 14th century, Villefranche, 6km (4 miles) east of Nice, is a lively fishing port located in a beautiful sheltered bay. The pretty harbour, with tall, pastel-coloured buildings, is lined by cafés and brasseries. Behind is the old town, running uphill, with stairs and narrow alleyways, including the vaulted rue Obscure. The impressive 16th-century fort was strengthened by the great military engineer Vauban. It houses the town hall, and contains some minor art collections. The fort also has an auditorium, and stages outdoor cinema and theatre shows in the summer.

A ring of medieval ramparts and gateways protected Vieux Vence (Old Vence). Much of the defence remains, most notably at the Porte du Peyra, a 15th-century fortified gate with 17th-century additions. Place du Peyra and place Clémenceau are charming tree-shaded open areas. The latter gives access to the former cathedral, dating from the 10th century but with Roman fragments and later additions. The latest of all, in the baptistery, is striking: a mosaic by Marc Chagall depicting Moses in the bulrushes.

The town has strong links with many painters and writers. In the 1920s it became an artistic haven, attracting the likes of Gide, Dufy and D H Lawrence, who died here in 1930 of tuberculosis.

Chapelle du Rosaire

Henri Matisse designed and decorated this chapel between 1947 and 1951. The starkness of his bold black-and-

Chapelle de St-Pierre-des-Pêcheurs

Inside this 14th-century chapel, once a sanctuary for local fishermen, are murals painted by Jean Cocteau in 1956.

Quai Courbet. Tel: 04 93 76 90 70. Open: Oct–May 10am–noon & 3–5pm; Jun–Sept Tue–Sun 10am–noon & 3–7pm. Admission charge.

Alpes-de-Haute-Provence

Provence's away-from-it-all département – and its least populated – is the meeting ground between Mediterranean and Alpine influences. Pastoral foothills in the south eventually rise into rocky mountain ranges, snowcapped for much of the year. Apart from developments along the Durance Valley, the Alpes-de-Haute-Provence is largely unaffected by change. Its rugged character and robust, grey-stoned mountain villages make it the least Provençal of the region's five départements.

Castellane

Castellane's location at the eastern approach of the Grand Canyon du Verdon (*see pp128–9*) guarantees a healthy number of summer visitors. Its market square, place Marcel-Sauvaire, is set against a backdrop of steep hills. The steepest of all is the huge rocky outcrop, looming over the town, which is topped by the little pilgrimage chapel of **Notre-Dame-du-Roc**. The 18th-century chapel is a 30-minute walk along a path that passes the Tour Pentagonale, a five-sided fortified tower that was part of the town's medieval defences.

Castellane is an excellent centre for outdoor pursuits, with equipment shops and agencies covering the whole sporting spectrum, from mountain biking to white-water rafting.
Castellane is 63km (39 miles) northwest of Grasse.

Digne-les-Bains

Digne's famous spa is hidden in a secluded, wooded valley a few kilometres from the centre. While the *thermes* have an ongoing air of prosperity, the town itself shows a few signs of neglect. The cathedral, a grim-looking hulk enlivened by a tall campanile, needs some care and attention. The open spaces of place du Général de Gaulle are much more visitor-friendly, though lacking the animated atmosphere of other French towns. But do not be discouraged by these negatives. Digne, which enjoys a beautiful, mountain-ringed location, is a restrained place with an understated charm typical of many spa towns.

Musée Alexandra David-Néel

The house of the fiercely individualistic Alexandra David-Néel recalls her fascination with all things Tibetan.
27 avenue du Maréchal-Juin. Tel: 04 92 31 32 38. www.alexandra-david-neel.org. Open (guided tours only): Jul–Sept daily 10am–6pm; Oct–Jun daily 10am–5pm. Admission charge.

Musée Gassendi

Located in an old 16th-century hospice, archaeology, art and natural history are all covered here.

64 boulevard Gassendi. Tel: 04 92 31 45 29. Open: Apr–Sept Tue–Sun 11am–7pm; Oct–Mar Tue–Sun 1.30–5.30pm. Admission charge.

Digne-les-Bains is 117km (73 miles) northwest of Grasse.

Entrevaux

This characterful Provençal town makes no secret of its strategic importance. You enter by crossing the fairy-tale Porte Royale, a remarkable fortified bridge over the River Var. But that is just the beginning, for the citadel that fulfils the serious defensive role is perched high on a rock above the rooftops, an eyrie from which it keeps a threatening, all-seeing eye on the valley.

Alpes-de-Haute-Provence

The original fortification was strengthened in the late 17th century by Vauban, Louix XIV's military architect, to defend this frontier town in France's disputes with Savoy. The only way up is along a zigzagging pathway cut into the rock. If you can't face the climb, then content yourself with Entrevaux's 17th-century cathedral which is built into the town's street-level defences. As a respite from Entrevaux's overpoweringly medieval air, you can retreat into the decidedly 20th-century little museum that celebrates the motor car.

Musée de la Poudrière open: daily 9am–6pm. Further details from the Office de Tourisme (tel: 04 93 05 46 73) and Town Hall (tel: 04 93 05 40 04). Entrevaux is on the N202, 72km (45 miles) northwest of Nice.

Forcalquier

This unexpectedly engaging small town lies at the heart of Provence between the Mediterranean and the Alps, a hilly, sunny area in which olive and beech trees grow side by side. Forcalquier has all the trappings of a long history – a ruined hilltop citadel, cathedral, wealth of other religious sites, Romanesque monuments, weathered Renaissance façades – but little of the fame enjoyed by other heritage-rich towns.

The town's Golden Age was in early medieval times when the counts of Forcalquier created an independent state which lasted for over a century. Unlike places such as Aix, in which every ancient feature is assiduously cherished, Forcalquier is not meticulous about preserving its past.

The medieval fortified town of Entrevaux looks over the River Var

The Couvent de la Visitation is an old convent and chapel of delicately carved stonework that have unceremoniously been converted into a town hall, museum – and cinema!

If you prefer your historic sites in their original state, then this is the place for you. Dominating place du Bourguet, the central square, is Notre-Dame-du-Marché, a large complex dating from the early 12th century.

The old town lies behind the cathedral, an area of 13th- to 18th-century houses that look their age. Place St-Michel's 16th-century fountain has an explicit carving demonstrating that medieval sexual practices in France deserve a mention in the *Kama Sutra*.

A short distance south of Forcalquier are two interesting places to visit – the Château de Sauvan and the Observatoire de Haute-Provence.

Forcalquier's Notre-Dame-de-Provence chapel dates from the 19th century

Château de Sauvan

This opulent 18th-century château, set in splendid grounds, looks like a refugee from the Loire Valley.
About 7km (4 miles) south of Forcalquier on the N100. Tel: 04 92 75 05 64. Open for guided tour only: Jul–Aug daily (except Sat) at 3.30pm; Sept–Jun Thur & Sun 3.30pm. Admission charge.

Couvent des Cordeliers

Forcalquier's 13th-century Franciscan monastery preserves its scriptorium, library, monastic hall and terraces.
Boulevard des Martyrs de la Résistance. Tel: 04 92 75 25 19. Open: for exhibitions daily 10am–2pm & 4–7pm. Admission charge.

Musée de Salagon

A museum housed in a medieval priory with gardens of rich botanical interest.
Prieuré de Salagon, Mane (3.5km/ 2 miles southwest of Forcalquier). Tel: 04 92 75 70 50. www.musee-de-salagon.com. Open: Feb–Apr, Oct & Dec daily 2–5pm; May & Sept daily 10am–12.30pm & 2–6.30pm; Jun–Aug daily 10am–7.30pm; Nov Sun only 2–5pm. Closed: Jan. Admission charge.

Observatoire de Haute-Provence

The National Centre for Scientific Research sited its observatory here because of the area's clear skies and lack of industrial pollution.

Walk under the arch of the Porte Saunerie to enter the old town of Manosque

Accessible via St-Michel l'Observatoire off the N100 southwest of Forcalquier. Tel: 04 92 76 69 69. www.centre-astro.fr. Open: Apr–Sept Wed 2–4pm; Oct–Mar Wed only one session at 3pm.

Forcalquier is 83km (52 miles) northeast of Aix-en-Provence.

Grand Canyon du Verdon
See pp128–9.

Manosque
This bustling town is set on a hillside above the wide Durance Valley. Not so long ago, only 5,000 people lived here: that figure has now quadrupled. A strategic location, good communications by autoroute, a nearby nuclear research centre and an enviable climate have turned Manosque into the archetypal Provençal boom town. Signs of affluence are everywhere: in the neatly refurbished streets, the solidly middle-income shops and the well-dressed populace.

Manosque's focus of interest lies within the relatively small area of the old town, defined by a circular one-way traffic system. You can enter on foot through Porte Saunerie, a tall, fortified gateway that looks like a disembodied castle tower. A short distance along the pedestrianised rue Grande is a plaque announcing the birthplace of Jean Giono (1895–1970), who wrote about the people and places of this part of Provence (*see p105*). A little further along rue Grande is the **Église St-Sauveur** with a handsome, plain façade and ornate wrought-iron campanile (a bell cage, built to withstand the *mistral* wind, which you see on churches and monuments all across Provence).

This is a town that rewards aimless wandering. You will come across many pleasing details: the shady fountains, the mellow stonework, the beautifully carved doorways (look out especially for the Renaissance carvings on the portal of Manosque's other church, the **Église Notre-Dame-de-Romigier**).

Centre Jean Giono
This museum and cultural centre focuses on the town's favourite son. *1 boulevard Elémir-Bourges. Tel: 04 92 70 54 55. www.centrejeangiono.com. Open: Apr–Sept Tue–Sun 9.30am–noon & 2–6pm; Oct–Mar Tue–Sat 2–6pm. Admission charge.*

Manosque is 50km (31 miles) northeast of Aix-en-Provence.

Santons

Folk art and religious faith come together in Provence in the Nativity scenes that occupy pride of place in the home at Christmas time. The figures, known as *santons* (little saints), are made of baked clay formed from plaster-cast moulds. They are painted in meticulous detail with acrylics and range from thimble-size to doll-size.

A town in miniature

These crèches are unique, for they contain not only the biblical figures of Jesus, Mary, Joseph, shepherds and Wise Men, but also a supporting cast representing people in a 19th-century Provençal town. Wearing clothes of that period, the *santons* depict a cross-section of society: farmers, fishermen, shopkeepers, teachers, businessmen, priests, and so on. There are sometimes more than a hundred figures on display, as well as intricately fashioned models of stone houses surrounding the stable. Twigs of rosemary and thyme depict trees, while hillsides are made out of pebbles and moss.

Spreading custom

The custom began in Marseille early in the 19th century, when the original *santonniers* (*santon* makers) modelled their figurines on the village characters portrayed in the Nativity plays known as *pastorales* and the ingenious *crèches parlantes* ('talking cribs' with speaking marionettes). The custom spread to neighbouring towns and villages and has since become a popular Provençal tradition. Marseille and the nearby city of Aix-en-Provence are still the *santon*-making centres of Provence, and a great *santon* fair is held in Marseille for two weeks each winter. Although especially linked to the festive season, *santons* can be bought at craft shops and fairs in Provence at any time of the year.

Colourful *santons* in 19th-century dress, now sold as souvenirs

Moustiers-Ste-Marie

Moustiers is invariably criticised for being a tourist trap. This is unfair. The criticisms, one suspects, are based on pure aesthetics: whereas some places along the coast are a lost cause, Moustiers could be even more attractive without the souvenir and gift shops.

Its location is breathtaking. The village is built into the side of a V-shaped ravine split by a rushing watercourse, a fairy-tale setting. In the town you will find pottery shops . . . and pottery shops . . . and pottery shops. Moustiers pottery has been famous for centuries. After a spell in the doldrums, the industry revived in the 1930s and now makes a thriving living off its glazed decorative ware.

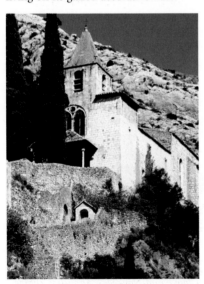

Spectacularly situated Moustiers has produced fine ceramics for centuries

Another reason for the village's popularity is its location at the western gateway to the Grand Canyon du Verdon (*see pp128–9*). In summer, congestion is a problem. The sensible thing to do is to come early or late in the day – or, better still, in the spring or autumn.

Exploration is a delight when you have the place to yourself. The pretty cobbled square above the church leads to a steep pathway that climbs high up the side of the ravine to a second religious site, the 12th-century **Chapelle Notre-Dame-de-Beauvoir**. Higher still, suspended on a 227m (745ft) long chain, is a famous curiosity – a man-sized star, supposedly placed there by a knight returning from the Crusades (the existing version, it should be pointed out, is 1957-vintage).

Musée de la Faïence (Pottery Museum)
Exhibits trace the history of Moustiers pottery.
Place du Presbytère. Tel: 04 92 74 61 64 (Office de Tourisme). Open: Apr–Oct Wed–Mon 9am–noon & 2–6pm; Nov–Dec & Feb–Mar Sat & Sun 2–5pm. Closed: Jan. Admission charge.

Moustiers-Ste-Marie is 48km (30 miles) south of Digne-les-Bains.

Riez

Neighbouring Moustiers-Ste-Marie grabs all the attention, leaving Riez to its fate as an obscure country town. The visitors who do come – accidentally or otherwise – will discover a great deal of antiquity, presented without any of the usual fuss or flourish. Riez was an important meeting of the ways for the Romans. Four Roman columns, the remnants of a temple, stand like a piece of surreal art in a field on the outskirts of town. The original Roman settlement was on the hill of Mont St-Maxime above, the site of a 17th-century chapel and a good viewpoint across the surrounding lavender fields.

Further echoes of Riez's former – and now faded – glory can be traced among the rich Renaissance façades along Grand-Rue, the early Christian baptistery next to the excavated site of the cathedral, and the grandly proportioned Hôtel de Ville (Town Hall), originally an episcopal palace. *Riez is 42km (26 miles) south of Digne-les-Bains.*

Sisteron

You need not be a military historian to understand Sisteron's strategic value. It grew up at a point where the Durance Valley funnels into a narrow defile between two enormous outcrops. Surmounting the western rock is an awesome, grey-stone citadel, guardian of a crucial gateway into Provence from the Alps.

The medieval citadel stands on a site that has been fortified for thousands of years. From the summit, high above the single bridge across the river, the citadel's grey mass is mirrored

ROUTE NAPOLÉON

After escaping from the island of Elba in March 1815, Napoleon landed at Golfe-Juan, marching northwards with a small band of followers to reclaim Paris. His route took him through Cannes, Mouans-Sartoux, St-Vallier-de-Thierry, Escragnolles and Castellane, where he crossed the Verdon by the now disused stone bridge. He was hardly greeted with open arms, and had to avoid Grasse, continuing on through the hills and mountains on stony, obscure tracks. It was not until he reached Gap that he began to regain some of his hero status.

His march through the mountains is commemorated by the winding N85, now known as the Route Napoléon, built in the 1930s.

by the outcrop of Rocher de la Baume opposite.

Below, tall dwellings line a maze of narrow streets known locally as *andrônes*. Instead of having the usual stone facing, they are rendered as protection against the cold draught from the Alps, giving Sisteron a robust mountain character rather than a sybaritic Mediterranean warmth.

Citadelle

Before it suffered Allied bombing in 1944, this towering fortress-cum-prison, built between the 13th and 17th centuries, was even more impressive. *Tel: 04 92 61 27 57. Open: Apr–May 9am–6.30pm; Jun 9am–7pm; Jul & Aug 9am–7.30pm; Sept–mid-Nov 9am–7pm. Closed: mid-Nov–Mar. Admission charge.*

Sisteron is 48km (30 miles) south of Gap.

Tour: Grand Canyon du Verdon

This natural spectacle is, in places, literally breathtaking. A giant slash cut deep into the earth's crust with heart-stopping 800m (2,625ft) drops and awesome vistas, this is one of the not-to-be-missed places on any visit to Provence. A road runs right around the canyon on both sides, thus allowing a convenient circular car tour of the entire spectacle.

With stops, the tour will take all day.

The only downside is its popularity. In summer, this route is a busy one. You will have to keep a wary eye not only on the road, which skirts some truly fearsome cliff edges, but also on other sightseeing motorists. Far better to come in the quieter autumn or spring, when you will have this stunning phenomenon almost entirely to yourself. You should also bear in mind that petrol stations in this remote corner are few and far between.

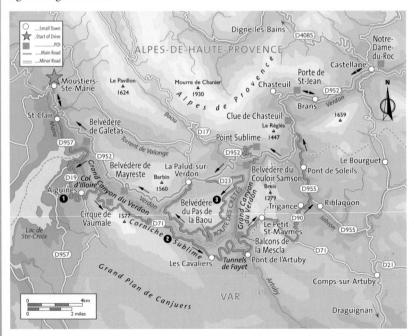

From Moustiers-Ste-Marie (see p126) take the D957 south, turning left on to the D19, which winds its way up through scrubland to Aiguines.

1 Aiguines

The pretty hilltop village of Aiguines enjoys wonderful views westwards to the Lac de Ste-Croix – a huge man-made sheet of unnaturally blue water fed by the River Verdon – and the strange, flat-topped plateau above it. From Aiguines, the serpentine road climbs up the Col d'Illoire for the first glimpse into the achingly deep canyon.

2 Corniche Sublime

The Col d'Illoire marks the start of the Corniche Sublime, which runs along the canyon's southern rim. Mossy, sheer-sided cliffs line the walls of a narrow defile carved by the Verdon. Along the corniche are noticeboards giving details of walks of different lengths and gradations into the canyon. Please note that some of these paths are very steep, so choose your trail carefully.
Beyond Les Cavaliers the road enters the Tunnels de Fayet, then crosses the River Artuby, a tributary of the Verdon. A short distance after the bridge, stop off at the Balcons de la Mescla, a viewpoint overlooking a great loop in the Verdon. This is your last glimpse of the gorge and river on the southern leg of the journey. Follow the D71 eastwards, turning left along the D90 towards Trigance, then left on the D955 for Pont de Soleils and the D952. Here, you can take a detour east to

A dizzying look down into the Grand Canyon du Verdon

Castellane (see p120). A few kilometres west of Pont de Soleils on the D952, take a short detour after the tunnel to the Belvédère du Couloir Samson, which ends in a deep cleft beside the rushing Verdon. Return to the D952 for the lofty viewpoint of 783m (2,569ft) Point Sublime. Continue westwards, turning left along the Route des Crêtes (D23).

3 Route des Crêtes

By now you may be tempted to miss the D23 loop, having had a surfeit of viewpoints. But on this tour, the best is kept for last. The Route des Crêtes is a must, eclipsing even the Corniche Sublime. There are so many breathtaking belvédères – and hair-raising hairpin bends – that it is impossible to describe them all (the 1,285m (4,216ft) high **Belvédère du Pas de la Baou** is particularly stunning). Rejoin the D952 at La Palud-sur-Verdon, passing the point where the river suddenly escapes from the canyon into the lake on the return to Moustiers.

Wildlife

The abundance of plant and animal life in Provence makes it a fascinating destination for naturalists. Wild rosemary and thyme grow on the pine-scented hillsides, while pyramidal cypress trees bring a darker, more dramatic accent of green to the surroundings. Vines flourish on sunny, stony slopes and plains, sometimes sharing a valley floor or hillside with olive groves.

Another distinct feature of Provence is the *garrigue* or *maquis*, names given to the dense undergrowth of stunted, hard-leafed evergreens, shrubs and bushes that harbour a wealth of animals. Orchids thrive in some areas, and edible fungi include truffles, which are gathered in Vaucluse with the aid of trained dogs. Palms and cacti add an exotic flavour.

The flowers of Provence attract butterflies of many species, and moths are to be found in profusion. Summer visitors among the bird population include the gaudy bee-eater, which feeds off insects it catches on the wing. The Camargue is a world-class nature reserve

Provence is a fascinating destination for naturalists

Exotic flamingoes are among the abundant wildlife in the region

renowned for its exceptional bird life, which includes pink flamingoes, marsh- and seabirds, waterfowl and birds of prey. Look out for egrets, perched on the back of cattle, feeding off the Camargue's itchy insect life.

Wild boars find shelter in the protective *garrigue*. Together with quails, pheasants, partridges – and practically anything else with a pair of wings or four legs – they attract the attention of the hunting-mad Provençals outside the protected areas. Other Provençal residents include beavers, many reptiles (tortoises, snakes, lizards) and even a few golden eagles in the remoter mountains.

You will not have to look too hard to find the cicada with its insistent click, a creature synonymous with a hot Provençal summer. And do not be too concerned if you see a scorpion scurrying out from under a rock – the French variety will, at worst, give you something like a wasp sting.

Getting away from it all

Anyone who has spent any time in Provence knows that it isn't just a region of perched villages, historic towns, ancient monuments, art, markets, coastal glitz and tempting food; it is also an area where landscape and nature both captivate the senses and dominate the way of life. The dramatic hills, mountains, rivers and gorges have not only been an inspiration for writers and artists, but are – for many – as much of a draw as the thronging coast and crowded cultural attractions.

Ardèche gorges

The gorges of the Ardèche get you away from Provence rather than away from it all. Only a short distance across the Rhône Valley from the Vaucluse, it would be pedantic in the extreme to ignore these gorges, one of the great natural wonders of France, even though they are technically outside the area. The gorges were formed by the River Ardèche, which has cut a deep channel through the limestone strata of a high plateau. They lie between Vallon-Pont-d'Arc (the main 'resort' town for the gorges) and **St-Martin-d'Ardèche** (a smaller tourist centre across the river from the clifftop fort at Aiguèze). The as-the-crow-flies distance between the two is a mere 18km (11 miles), which almost trebles when you follow the serpentine road that imitates the convoluted, looping progress of the river.

There are two ways of seeing the gorges. You can drive the corniche road, the D290, which has many spectacular viewpoints along the way. Access by foot into the deepest recesses of the gorge is impossible from these high *belvédères*: you will have to be content to stand and gaze. The only easy access to river level is at the beginning and end of the gorges, where there are popular swimming and sunbathing 'beach' areas.

The second method, by canoe, is far more rewarding. Canoe hire is extremely well organised from the two main centres, Vallon-Pont-d'Arc and St-Martin, with transport laid on for the outward or return leg of the journey. Make sure that you get good advice about the different sections of the river. Some parts are calm and easy, so little or no previous experience is required (though you must be able to swim!). Others, involving rapids, should only be tackled by the more experienced. You will be given tuition if necessary and full equipment (life jackets, waterproof containers, etc). Canoes can be hired for anything from half a day to two days (overnight camping is permitted). Water conditions range from calm to fast-flowing. The best time for novices is between June and August, when conditions are at their best and other canoeists are present in reassuringly high numbers. As an alternative to the do-it-yourself approach, there are trips piloted by experienced boatmen (ask at Vallon-Pont-d'Arc's Office de Tourisme for details, *tel: 04 75 88 04 01*).

The journey starts at Vallon-Pont-d'Arc. Within a few kilometres you will come across the Ardèche's most photographed feature, the famous **Pont-d'Arc**, a natural arch 34m (112ft) high and 59m (194ft) wide (also accessible from the D290). From here, the river is shut away for 30km (19 miles), looping and meandering within an inaccessible chasm lined with towering walls of rock rising to 300m (984ft).

The D290 runs along the northern rim of the gorges. Its most spectacular section is the **Haute Corniche** (High Corniche) about two-thirds

---

CANOE HIRE

There are many operators offering more or less the same service. Here are two:
Alpha Bateaux *Pierre Peschier, route des Gorges, Vallon-Pont-d'Arc. Tel: 04 75 88 08 29.*
Aventure Canoes *Place du Marché, Vallon-Pont-d'Arc. Tel: 04 75 37 18 14.*

---

of the way along to St-Martin. **Belvédère de la Madeleine**, a short walk from the road, and the roadside **Belvédère de la Cathédrale** are tremendous viewpoints overlooking the highest part of the gorge.

Aven d'Orgnac

This is one of Europe's finest showcaves, and also houses a prehistory museum. *Near Barjac south of the gorges. Tel: 04 75 38 65 10. Open: Apr–Jun & Sept daily 10am–5.30pm; Jul & Aug till 6.30pm; Feb & Mar daily 10.30am–noon & 2–4.45pm; Oct–mid-Nov daily 9.30am–noon & 2–5.15pm. Closed: mid-Nov–Jan. Guided tours only. Admission charge.*

The clifftop fort at Aiguèze stands above the River Ardèche

Aven de Marzal

This attraction offers tours of an underground cave system, museum and prehistoric 'zoo' with life-size dinosaurs. *Near St-Remèze, north of the gorges. Tel: 04 75 04 12 45. Open: Apr–Sept daily 9am–6pm; Jul–Aug daily 10am–7.30pm. Closed: Oct–Mar. Admission charge.*

Abbaye du Thoronet

This secluded abbey lies hidden in the Forêt de la Darboussière (Darboussière Forest) north of the A8 autoroute in the Haut-Var. Together with the Abbaye de Sénanque (*see p37*) and the Abbaye de Silvacane (*see p48*), it is one of the 'three Provençal sisters' founded by the Cistercians in the 12th century. The earliest – and possibly the finest – of the three, it bears all the hallmarks of the Cistercians' ascetic approach. Its austere simplicity combined with harmonious proportions gives it a rare beauty.
The most straightforward approaches are either via Brignoles in the west or Draguignan in the east. Tel: 04 94 60 43 90. Open: Apr–Sept Mon–Sat 10am–6.30pm, Sun 10am–noon & 2–6.30pm; Oct–Mar Mon–Sat 10am–1pm & 2–5pm, Sun 10am–noon & 2–5pm. Admission charge.

Massif des Maures

If you want to escape from the crowded coast between Hyères and St-Tropez, then head inland into the densely wooded, sparsely populated hills of the Massif des Maures, the oldest mountain range in Provence. Its name derives from the Provençal *maouro*, used to describe this upland's dark cover of cork oak, chestnut and pine. There

The church at La Garde-Freinet

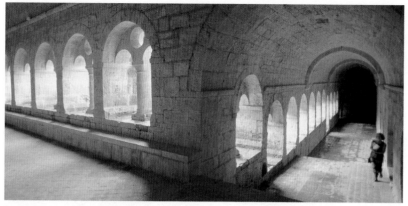

Long, silent corridors of the Abbaye du Thoronet

are a few tortuous, twisting roads through the mountains, though the Maures – which rise to over 700m (2,297ft) – are best explored on foot (the cross-country GR9 path takes in most of the high ridges).

La Garde-Freinet, the tiny 'capital' of the Maures, was France's main cork-producing town in the 19th century. It still makes a living from the local cork oak, though nowadays it has diversified into cork craft ornaments for tourists. Its ruined medieval castle marks the site of an earlier stronghold occupied by the feared Saracens.

To the southwest, in the heart of the Maures, is the ancient village of Collobrières. Confectionery made from sweet chestnuts has now replaced its cork industry. A mountain pass northwards climbs to **Notre-Dame-des-Anges**, a pilgrimage site almost at the summit of the Maures, which enjoys predictably panoramic views.

Montagne de Lure

This mountain, a near sister to the slightly higher Mont Ventoux (*see pp46–7*), rises to 1,826m (5,991ft) above Sisteron and the Durance Valley. Not as well served by roads (nor as heavily featured in guidebooks) as Mont Ventoux, its wooded slopes and barren summit offer a real chance of escape.

The mountain can be approached from north or south. For a north-south tour, leave Sisteron on the N85, taking the D946 through the pretty Jabron Valley. Then turn left on to the D53 (closed in winter), which winds along the base of a natural amphitheatre for about 5km (3 miles) before it starts the ascent of Lure's forested slopes.

Aire de St-Robert is an attractive picnic area, the starting point for a number of woodland walks. From here, the road surface becomes poorer for a few kilometres, though the views soon make the effort worthwhile: through

The limestone hills of the Luberon provide diverse landscapes

the trees you will catch glimpses of the snowcapped Alps as well as the Forêt Domaniale du Jabron, which covers Lure's thickly wooded foothills.

At the 1,597m (5,240ft) high Col du Pas de la Graille, trees give way to patchy moorland, bare rock and even better views. If you are feeling energetic, you can park the car here and follow a footpath the final few kilometres to the summit of Signal de Lure.

The summit, like that of Ventoux, bristles with strange-looking telecommunications equipment. A dizzy 360-degree panorama seems to encompass most of southern France, from the jagged Alps to the plateaux and plains leading down to the coast.

The descent of the mountain is on the wider D113 to sleepy St-Etienne (nervous drivers might prefer to go up as well as down on this road).

Parc Naturel Régional du Luberon

The Luberon Regional Natural Park, bounded in the south by the Durance River and in the north by the beginnings of the Vaucluse Plateau, is a 60km (37-mile) long chain of mountains rising to over 1,100m (3,609ft). The park consists of two parts: the Petit Luberon in the west near Cavaillon, a rugged area of gorges and ravines, and the higher Grand Luberon between Apt and Manosque in the east.

In the hierarchy of protected areas in France, a Regional Natural Park comes second to a National Park. The Luberon was declared a Regional Park in 1977 because of the special nature of its landscapes and local traditions. Unlike a National Park, where preservation of a wilderness area is paramount, a Regional Park attempts to balance conservation with appropriate sustainable commercial activities, including tourism.

In many ways, the Luberon takes its character from its villages, which are mostly strung out below its long spine of mountains. Human settlement, as much as natural forces, has shaped the Luberon's beautiful landscapes. Its hilltop villages (familiar to readers of Peter Mayle's *A Year in Provence*) are surrounded by vast patches of cultivated land, its higher pastures are tended by sheep farmers, and its ochre cliffs have been mined for dye.

The Luberon's fractured landscapes of high limestone cliffs, scrub, shrub and forest display an absolutely amazing diversity. Sunny south-facing slopes are clothed in an aromatic Mediterranean vegetation, while oaks grow along its cooler, more humid northern escarpment. Diversity is the keynote here, for the Luberon's rich flora and fauna include holm and downy oak, cedar, pine, cypress, rosemary, honeysuckle, lavender, eagle, owl, wild boar and beaver.

Full information on the park, including details of walking and cycle routes, is available at the Maison du Parc Naturel Régional du Luberon in Apt (*see pp22–3*). Pages 24–5 feature a car tour of the Petit Luberon.

Parc National du Mercantour

In terms of outright environmental protection, this National Park is one notch up on the Luberon Regional Park. The Mercantour, roughly 90km by 30km (56 miles by 19 miles), runs close to the French/Italian border more or less from Sospel to Barcelonnette, embracing big-league mountains consistently in the 2,500–3,000m (8,200–9,850ft) range. Most of the park lies in the Alpes-Maritimes, with a small northern section in the Alpes-de-Haute-Provence.

Exploration of this challenging wilderness should not be taken lightly. Walkers should always expect the worst: parts of the park have a long, snowy winter that can last from October to June. Even in summer nothing is predictable, for weather conditions can change alarmingly in a short space of time and from valley to valley.

The Mercantour was Italian territory until after World War II, when it was ceded to France and became a nature reserve. Its highest mountain is Mont Pelat, a 3,051m (10,010ft) peak that rises above Lac d'Allos, a mountain lake itself at over 2,200m (7,218ft) and accessible by road from Allos. This northern corner of the park also contains the memorable mountain road over the 2,802m (9,193ft) high Col de la Bonette, which drops down into the Tinée Valley.

However, the Mercantour's acknowledged centrepiece lies further southeast at the **Val des Merveilles**.

Getting away from it all

The only access to this remote valley is by foot. From St-Dalmas-de-Tende on the N204 north of Saorge (*see pp114–15*) the D91 leads west for about 8km (5 miles) to Les Mesches, starting point for a 10km (6-mile) footpath into this dramatic valley with its mysterious Bronze Age rock carvings.

The Mercantour's wildlife could fill a book. More than half of the 4,000 species of wildflowers growing in France are found here, including rare saxifrage, lily and orchid. The park, of course, is the perfect habitat for eagles, buzzards, falcons and kestrels. Other species at home here include chamois, ibex and wild boar.

Réserve Naturelle Géologique de Haute Provence

Eighteen separate sites centred around Digne-les-Bains were declared Nature Reserves in 1984 in an attempt to protect them from damage. The earth's geological record is contained within this spread of valuable sites, which stretches from near Castellane in the south to Barles in the north, a distance of about 50km (31 miles). They contain deposits of plant life, ammonite skeletons from the time when sea covered the Alps, and even traces of bird footprints left some 30 million years ago.

The Mercantour National Park

Public access to the sites is controlled. Information on guided visits is available from the Centre de Géologie (open daily) at St-Benoît about 4km (2¹/₂ miles) from the centre of Digne on the D900. This is a research establishment with exhibition rooms open to the public. *Tel: 04 92 336 70 70. Open: Apr–Jun & Sept–Oct daily 9am–noon & 2–5.30pm (till 4.30pm on Fri); Jul & Aug Mon–Fri 9am–1pm & 2–7pm, Sat–Sun 10.30am–12.30pm & 2–7pm; Nov–Mar Mon–Fri 9am–noon & 2–5.30pm.*

Tourtour

Tourtour is typical of the enchanting Provençal villages you invariably stumble across when you wander off the main highways. To find Tourtour, a village in the empty northern spaces of the Haut-Var, take the D77 (off the D557 west of Draguignan), a road that winds up a beautiful wooded escarpment.

The village, a picturesque jumble of vaulted archways, wrought-iron balconies, ancient stone staircases and shadowy passageways – with a fountain at almost every corner – would by now have been buried in souvenir shops were it nearer to the coast. Tourtour's lack of pretension is summed up by the way in which its post office is housed in a 16th-century bastion complete with four enormous round corner towers. Although the village shows signs of

An ammonite fossil

infiltration by craft galleries and expensive eating places, they do not yet dilute a convincingly authentic atmosphere.

From the Église St-Denis, Tourtour's lofty location at over 600m (1,969ft) becomes apparent. The church occupies a splendid viewpoint looking southwards to the sea, a panorama fully explained by a helpful *table d'orientation.*

Shopping

Best buys in Provence are undoubtedly its local crafts and artefacts. You will not even have to go into a conventional shop for some things. Family potteries, for example, often sell their wares beside the road; sometimes you will find fields the size of football pitches stacked full of kitchenware, urns, plates and pots. At the other end of the spectrum are expensive craft shops and galleries. Some villages, especially the 'perched villages' in southern Provence, have been completely taken over by such shops.

Items on sale include the miniature figures known as *santons* (*see p125*), toilette products made from local lavender and herbs, a wide range of pottery, leatherwork, honey, hand-woven baskets and the brightly patterned fabrics of traditional Provençal design. The best – but most expensive – place for the latter is the Souleiado or les Olivades range of stores. Some towns specialise in particular products. Grasse is famous for its perfume, Biot for its exquisite glassware, and Vallauris for its colourful pottery.

Where to shop

There seems to be a standard pattern to the larger Provençal towns. The town centre is reserved for the smaller shops, while on the outskirts are sprawling complexes that contain the hypermarkets, motor accessory stores, and the large do-it-yourself and furniture outlets. While the hypermarkets are short on ambience,

they are extremely convenient. In addition to the vast supermarket that forms the core of the centre, you will also find a range of other shops – selling everything from sports goods to musical instruments – all under one roof.

Prices

Do not try to haggle over prices – bargaining will get you nowhere in Provence. The exception to this rule is the outdoor flea market or antique sale. Here you can often negotiate a reduction of the asking price.

VAT

The Value Added Tax in France, known as TVA (*taxe à la valeur ajoutée*), is incorporated in the price of almost every item or meal. It varies slightly according to the category of product but is most widely applied at the 19.6 per cent level. VAT is 5.5 per cent for many food items, and in 2009 VAT was reduced on restaurant meals (but not wine). However, restaurants aren't obliged to pass this saving on to the diner, and it is likely to be a temporary measure. Visitors from non-EU countries may, in some cases, be eligible for a TVA refund if the goods are taken out of the country within 90 days of being purchased. To facilitate this process, some stores offer an 'export sales invoice' (*bordereau* in French), which you must complete to make the claim, and both goods and *bordereau* must be shown to customs officials at the port or airport of departure. Note that not all shops offer this service, and others impose a minimal fee for the extra paperwork.

Opening hours

Shop hours in Provence respect the sanctity of the midday meal. Apart from the big stores and supermarkets, most shops close between noon and 2pm, though in compensation many stay open until quite late (6 or 7pm). Many towns and villages observe half-day closing some time during the week. Conventional 'high-street' shops are closed on Sunday, though shops aimed at the visitor market – craft shops, galleries, etc – usually remain open, especially in the popular tourist areas.

SPECIALITY SHOPS
Aix-en-Provence
Santon Fouque
This leading maker of *santons* has a shop and workshop.
65 cours Gambetta. Tel: 04 42 26 33 38.

La Victoire
Vibrant, high-quality Provençal fabrics and other items.
34 rue Vauvenargues. Tel: 04 42 23 14 36.

Arles
Carnet de Voyage
Souvenirs and local products.
4 bis rue de la Calade. Tel: 04 90 96 17 95.
La Main Qui Pense
Pottery by the talented ceramicist Cécile Cayrol.
15 rue Tour de Fabre. Tel: 04 90 18 24 58.

Avignon
There are many small speciality shops in the maze of narrow streets off the main rue de la République. One of the city's most stylish and exclusive shopping streets is rue Joseph Vernet.
La Bouteillerie du Palais des Papes
In the Palais des Papes (free entry to the shop), carefully selected Côte du Rhône wines. Tastings, too. *Tel: 04 90 27 50 85.*

A shop sells dried flowers and fruits

Délices du Luberon
Local food products.
20 place du Change. Tel: 04 90 84 03 58.
Mallard
High-quality chocolate, pastries, sweets
and ice cream.
32 rue des Marchands. Tel: 04 90 82 42 38.
Souleiado
Traditional fabrics.
19 rue Joseph Vernet. Tel: 04 90 86 32 05.

Biot
La Verrière de Biot
Biot's distinctive bubbled glassware is
made and sold here.
5 chemin des Combes. Tel: 04 93 65 03 00.

Cannes
For the latest designer fashions with
expense no object, there's none to beat
the exclusive boutiques (Chanel,
Yves Saint Laurent, etc) along Cannes'
La Croisette. Rue d'Antibes and
rue Meynadier are two other
fashionable shopping streets.

Attractively packaged *herbes de Provence*

Eze
Parfumerie Fragonard
This large perfumery, soap and
cosmetics factory sells its products
directly to the public.
*On the Moyenne Corniche (middle coast
road) between Nice and Monaco.
Tel: 04 93 41 05 05.*

Fontaine-de-Vaucluse
Fabrication Artisanale de Papier, Vallis Clausa
Water-powered machinery helps in the
production of handmade paper, which is
used in a wide range of prints and maps.
*Chemin de la Fontaine.
Tel: 04 90 20 34 14. www.vallis-clausa.com*

Grasse
You are spoilt for choice shopping for
perfume – and you should be able to
purchase the perfume at factory prices.
Parfumerie Fragonard
*20 boulevard Fragonard. Tel: 04 93 36 44
65. Also 2km (1^1/$_4$ miles) from the town
centre on the route de Cannes. Tel: 04 93
40 12 04. www.fragonard.com*
Parfumerie Galimard
*73 route de Cannes. Tel: 04 93 09 20 00.
www.galimard.com*
Parfumerie Molinard
*60 boulevard Victor-Hugo.
Tel: 04 93 36 01 62. www.molinard.com*

Marseille
La Maison du Pastis
Pastis is very much the local tipple, and
here you can find over 100 pastis and
absinthe products.

108 quai du Port. Tel: 04 91 90 86 77.
www.lamaisondupastis.com
Santons Marcel Carbonel
This shop and workshop, run by a
famous *santonnier*, also has a small
museum.
47 rue Neuve Ste-Catherine.
Tel: 04 91 54 26 58.
www.santonsmarcelcarbonel.com
Savonnerie la Licorne
One of the few handmade soap
producers left in Marseille. You can also
learn about how the soap is made.
30 Cours Julien. Tel: 04 96 12 00 91.

Menton
Au Pays du Citron
Food and drink products made from
local lemons.
24 rue Saint-Michel. Tel: 04 92 09 22 85.
www.aupaysducitron.fr

Monaco
The best shopping areas are: the cluster
of streets in La Vieille-Ville; in La
Condamine, the pedestrian area of rue
Grimaldi and rue Princesse Caroline;
in Monte Carlo, in the Centre
Comercial La Métropole, boulevard des
Moulins and the Galerie du Park-Pale
in avenue de la Costa; and in
Fontvieille, the Centre Comercial in
avenue Prince-Héreditaire Albert.

Nice
You will find most of the major stores
along avenue Jean-Médecin, the main
shopping thoroughfare, along avenue
de Verdun, and the more upmarket

Masséna quarter, a pedestrianised area
of chic boutiques.

Confiserie du Vieux Nice
Crystallised fruit is a speciality of Nice.
There are guided tours of this
confectionery, and a wide selection of
its colourful range of products.
14 quai Papacino.
Tel: 04 93 55 43 50.

Nîmes
Les Olivades
Specialists in Provençal fabrics.
4 place Maison Carrée.
Tel: 04 66 21 01 31.

St-Rémy-de-Provence
Les Olivades
Place de la Mairie.
Tel: 04 90 92 00 80.
Souleiado
Traditional Provençal fabrics –
garments and accessories.
2 avenue de la Résistance.
Tel: 04 90 92 45 90.

Salon-de-Provence
Chocolaterie Le Nostradamus
Freshly made chocolates and sweets.
122 avenue 22 Août.
Tel: 04 90 53 13 97.

Séguret
Philippe Fournier
The shop is small, just like the
miniature *santons* it sells – but there is
a wonderful choice of items.
Rue Poternes. Tel: 04 90 46 91 35.

Finely crafted baskets for sale

Tourrettes-sur-Loup
Confiserie des Gorges-sur-Loup
Sweet-making is elevated to a fine art at this candied fruit factory and shop.
Le Pont du Loup.
Tel: 04 93 59 32 91.

Vallauris
Céramiques Natoli
This pottery shop gives demonstrations in pot-throwing as well as selling its wares.
Avenue Jérôme-Massier/boulevard des deux Vallons.
Tel: 04 93 64 02 36.

MARKETS
Provence's open-air markets are the best free show in Provence. All the big towns and many villages hold weekly – sometimes daily – markets. The streets are crammed full of stalls, and the mingling aromas of lavender, herbs, ripe cheese, olives, fresh fish and chicken roasting on a spit waft through the crowds. In summer a variety of street entertainers soon gather large audiences for impromptu performances of everything from organ grinding to juggling.

Please note that, in most cases, the markets are mornings only. By noon, the stallholders are beginning to shut up shop.

Aix-en-Provence
Daily fruit and vegetable market (place Richelme); flower market on Tuesday, Thursday and Saturday (place de l'Hôtel-de-Ville); fruit, vegetable and herb market on Tuesday, Thursday and Saturday (place des Prêcheurs); antiques market Tuesday, Thursday and Saturday mornings (place de Verdun).

Antibes
Daily general market (cours Masséna), closed Mon except July & August.

Apt
Tuesday in cours Lauze de Perrer.

Arles
Wednesday and Saturday, boulevard des Lices.

Avignon
Covered food market Tuesday to Sunday mornings (Les Halles, place Pie). Flea market on Sunday mornings (place des Carmes).

Barjols
Crafts market Tuesday to Saturday.

Bédoin
Monday.

Cannes
Daily general market
(Marché Forville).
Closed Monday. Bric-a-
brac market on Saturday
(allées de la Liberté).

Carpentras
Friday.

Châteauneuf-du-Pape
Friday.

Digne
Wednesday and
Saturday.

Draguignan
Daily food market. Flea
market first Saturday
every month.

Fréjus
Wednesday and Saturday.

Gordes
Tuesday arts and crafts
market.

Grasse
Provençal market
Tuesday to Sunday.

L'Îsle-sur-la-Sorgue
Thursday. Food and
antiques on Sunday.

Le Lavandou
Thursday.

Manosque
Saturday.

Marseille
Fish market daily except
Sunday (quai des
Belges).

Menton
Daily covered food
market (quai de
Monléon). Bric-a-brac
market on Friday (place
aux Herbes).

Monaco
Daily market (place
d'Armes, Monte Carlo).

Moustiers-Ste-Marie
Friday.

Nice
Daily, except Monday,
cours Saleya. Bric-a-brac
sold on Monday.

Nîmes
Monday flower and
antiques market.

Orange
Bric-a-brac market on
Thursday (place des
Cordeliers).

St-Rémy-de-Provence
Wednesday and
Saturday.

St-Tropez
Tuesday and Saturday.

Stes-Maries-de-la-Mer
Monday and Friday.

Salon-de-Provence
Wednesday.

Sanary-sur-Mer
Daily market.

Sault
Wednesday.

Sisteron
Wednesday and Saturday.

Toulon
Daily general market.

Vaison-la-Romaine
Tuesday. Sunday morning
in July and August.

A wonderful range of pottery

Crafts

The variety and quality of craftwork in Provence are evidence of a region in which folk art has achieved a high status. Craft traditions can be traced back at least as far as Roman times, for pottery workshops and kilns of the 1st century AD have been unearthed near Marseille.

Pottery and glass

The cheapest pottery produced today is called *terre rouge* after the reddish-brown colour it derives from the local red clay. Family workshops turn out jugs, bowls, pots and tiles, which are often sold at the roadside. The more decorative *faïence* style of pottery, first brought to France from Italy in the 16th century, has an enamel porcelain-like finish. Once found only in the homes of the wealthy, its appeal has since broadened considerably. *Grès* pottery, made from the grey clays of central France, lends itself to art pottery because of its hardness.

Provence's crafts are many and varied

Indiennage, the vibrant printed cottons of Provence

Another ancient craft has been brought to perfection in the town of Biot, where a unique method is employed to produce swirls of bubbles in clear or coloured blown glass.

Printed cottons

The vibrant printed cottons of Provence, known as *indiennage* because of their Indian influence, were first produced in the 17th century and have kept their strong appeal over the years. Traditionally they provided the humble shawl for generations of Provençal women, but they have now ventured upmarket and are used for interior decoration, fashion garments and shirts. Their brilliant colours and sharply defined patterns capture the essence of life in this sun-soaked region.

Contemporary crafts

The crafts scene in Provence is by no means entirely rooted in traditional folk art. An influx of artists since the 1950s has extended the range of crafts from the earthy to the eclectic, as a visit to almost any gallery will demonstrate. Tradition now coexists with innovation across a whole spectrum of crafts, embracing everything from woven murals and wooden toys to scented soaps and alternative toiletries.

Entertainment

Provence is essentially an open-air region. In northern Provence – apart from the main towns and cities – the sleepy, rural economy does not lend itself to frenetic entertainment when the lights go down. By 10pm, apart from when lively local fêtes are taking place, this part of Provence is soundly asleep. In the south, of course, it is just the opposite. Along the Riviera, the resorts buzz with life day and night.

CAFÉ SOCIETY

Everybody becomes part of the café society when in Provence. But there is a pecking order. You can enjoy a coffee or soft drink and watch the world go by in the main square of a humble country town, or pose conspicuously in a celebrated watering place along the coast where the next table just might be occupied by someone famous.

And you will pay for the fame-by-association. Even in ordinary cafés, prices for drinks are high. In the top spots, they are quite outrageous.

Aix-en-Provence

Cours Mirabeau is the street for pavement cafés and promenading. **Les Deux Garçons** (*53 cours Mirabeau*), with its gilt panelling, mirrors and ambience of a more languorous age, attracts an arty crowd.

Arles

The delightful little square – straight out of Van Gogh – known as the place du

Forum is lined with cafés. **Apostrophe** is one of the smarter ones. There are larger cafés along the boulevard des Lices.

Cannes

You will need a healthy bank balance to enjoy this resort to the full. Not only are the beaches and the film festival internationally famous, but one of the many attractive spots is **Mocca**, a bar/café open late (*1 boulevard de La Croisette*). The place to be seen during the film festival is the terrace bar of the **Carlton Hotel**.

Monaco

Expect to pay whopping prices anywhere around Monte Carlo's place du Casino, the meeting place of the high rollers. Prices are a little more sensible – but only just – in the old town of Monaco-Ville across the harbour.

St-Tropez

The cafés (Senequier and Le Gorille are two of the most famous) along the quai Jean-Jaurès and quai Suffren are the places from which to see it all – the yachts, parading crowds and ostentatious displays of wealth.

CASINOS

Unsuccessful gamblers can blame it all on Monte Carlo, for it was here, in 1865, that the Riviera's first casino opened.

To add insult to injury, some casinos now impose an admission charge – so you have to pay in order to lose money! Many casinos restrict entry to those 21 and over.

You will need your passport – and check the dress code. Many casinos have good restaurants.

Antibes
La Siesta
With a restaurant, bar and disco (weekends).
Route du Bord de la Mer – in the direction of Nice.
Tel: 04 93 33 31 31.

Beaulieu-sur-Mer
Casino de Beaulieu-sur-Mer
One of the oldest casinos on the coast, with a *belle époque* interior.

4 rue Fernand-Dunan.
Tel: 04 93 76 48 00.

Cannes
Casino Croisette
Part of the Palais des Festivals complex, modernised in 2009. With a view of the old port.
Jetée Albert-Edouard/La Croisette.
Tel: 04 92 98 78 60.
Les Princes Casino Barrière
50 boulevard La Croisette.
Tel: 04 97 06 18 50.

Cassis
Casino Barrière de Cassis
Avenue du Professeur Leriche.
Tel: 04 42 01 78 32.

Juan-les-Pins
Eden Casino
A modern building on the seafront.
Boulevard Baudoin.
Tel: 04 92 93 71 71.

Menton
Casino Barrière de Menton
With restaurant (good value at lunchtime), disco and bars.
Avenue Félix-Fauré.
Tel: 04 92 10 16 16.

Monaco
Casino de Monte-Carlo
Perhaps the most famous casino in the world, opened in 1865.
Place du Casino.
Tel: (377) 98 06 21 21.

Charles Garnier rebuilt the casino at Monte Carlo

Casino Sun
Fairmont Hotel, 12
avenue des Spélugues.
Tel: (337) 98 06 12 12.

Nice
Casino Ruhl
Two restaurants, two bars
and 300 slot machines.
1 promenade des Anglais.
Tel: 04 97 03 12 22.

St-Raphaël
Casino Barrière
Square de Grand.
Tel: 04 98 11 17 77.

DISCOS, CLUBS, BARS
Venues tend to come and
go as fashions change.
These are some of the
best-known places.

Aix-en-Provence
Le Scat Club
Live music.
Open from 11.30pm
(closed: Sun & Mon).
11 rue de la Verrerie.
Tel: 04 42 23 00 23.

Antibes/
Juan-les-Pins
Le Crystal
Large piano bar (a café
during the day) with
plenty of outdoor tables.
Avenue Georges Gallice.
Tel: 04 93 61 02 51.

Pam Pam
Lively venue specialising
in cocktails.
137 boulevard Wilson.
Tel: 04 93 61 11 05.

La Siesta
In a casino, disco open
weekends only.
Route du Bord de Mer in
the direction of Nice.
Tel: 04 93 33 31 31.

Voom-Voom
1 boulevard de la Pinède.
Tel: 04 92 93 90 90.

Avignon
Palais Royal
Restaurant with cabaret.
Place de l'Amirande.
Tel: 04 90 14 02 54.
www.palaisroyal.net

Le Red Zone
Bar and disco with a
young crowd.
25 rue Carnot.
Tel: 04 90 27 02 44.

Cannes
Le Bâoli
The best-known disco in
Cannes.
Port Pierre Canto, bd de
la Croisette. Tel: 04 93 43
03 43. Closed: Nov–Apr.

Upstairs
Young and smart.
13 rue Docteur Gérard
Monod.
Tel: 06 21 02 37 49.

Monaco
Jimmy'z
Legendary and expensive
nightclub at Le Sporting
Club de Monaco.
Avenue Princesse Grace.
Tel: (377) 92 16 22 77.
Open: Wed–Sun 10.30pm
onwards.
Closed: Nov–Easter.

Le Saphir
The Fairmont hotel
bar is open round the
clock. Piano music at
night.
12 avenue des Spélugues.
Tel: (377) 93 50 65 00.

Nice
De Klomp
A Dutch-style pub.
8 rue Mascoïnat.
Tel: 04 93 92 42 85.

Le Grande Escurial
One of the Côte d'Azur's
largest discos.
29 rue Alphonse Karr.
Tel: 04 93 82 37 66.

Wayne's
Live music, karaoke and
theme nights.
15 rue de la Préfecture.
Tel: 04 93 13 46 99.

St-Tropez
Le Papagayo
One of the most famous
clubs in town. Small,
lively and expensive.

Résidence du Nouveau-Port. Tel: 04 94 97 95 95.
Open: until 5am.
Closed: winter.

Les Caves du Roy
The famous disco of the Byblos hotel. It can get very crowded in summer, despite the price.
Avenue Paul Signac.
Tel: 04 94 97 16 02.
Closed: Nov–Mar.

THEATRE AND MUSIC

A wide range of performances takes place throughout Provence. Some of the most atmospheric and popular are held in the open air in Provence's Roman amphitheatres.

Aix-en-Provence

Le Grand Théâtre de Provence
Music and opera.
380 avenue Max Juvénal.
Tel: 04 42 91 69 69.
www.grandtheatre.fr

Le Pavillon Noir
Home of the Ballet Preljocaj dance company.
530 avenue Mozart.
Tel: 04 42 93 48 00.

Théâtre Jeu de Paume
17 rue Opéra.
Tel: 04 42 99 12 00.

Arles

Théâtre Antique
Rue du Cloître.
Tel: 04 90 49 36 74.

Avignon

Opéra Théâtre d'Avignon
Place de l'Horloge.
Tel: 04 90 82 42 42.

Marseille

Opéra Municipal
2 rue Molière.
Tel: 04 91 55 11 10.

Monaco

Opéra de Monte-Carlo
Designed by Charles Garnier.
Atrium du Casino, Place du Casino.
Tel: (337) 98 06 28 28.

Théâtre Princesse Grace
12 avenue d'Ostende.
Monte Carlo.
Tel: (337) 93 25 32 27.

Nice

Acropolis
Palais des Congrès,
1 esplanade Kennedy.
Tel: 04 93 92 83 00.

Opéra de Nice
4 rue St-François-de-Paul.
Tel: 04 92 17 40 40.

Palais Nikaia
Music performances from all genres.
163 rue de Grenoble.
Tel: 04 92 29 31 26.

Théâtre de Nice
Esplanade Victoires.
Tel: 04 93 13 90 90.

Orange

Théâtre Antique
Place des Frères-Mounet.
Tel: 04 90 51 17 60.

Toulon

Opéra de Toulon
Boulevard de Strasbourg.
Tel: 04 94 92 70 78.

Beaulieu-sur-Mer casino

Property hunting

The anecdotal accounts of writer Peter Mayle about how he set up home in the Luberon were a catalyst in an already-growing trend for northerners to flock south in search of sun, beautiful scenery and *la belle vie française*. Thanks to the popularity of his books, a subtle shift in expatriate focus took place from the historically popular Côte d'Azur and the Dordogne to Provence and the Luberon. Today, some 20 years later, there are no bargains left; no small

The picturesque Venasque

'ruins in need of restoration', no barns or outhouses suitable for inexpensive modification.

Prices in Provence have rocketed, and the locals know full well the value of their property. Having said that, this does not mean that there is no property available: far from it. There are probably far more property deals now than 20 years ago, but bargains are part of the past. To find a suitable second home, a house in which to live annually or a working farm or *gîte* requires considerable planning and probably as much – if not more – finance as a similar venture in Great Britain or other parts of Europe.

If you are not ready to take a research trip to Provence, then the Internet is a good place to start looking at prices and types of property. Follow that up through contact with an accredited *agent immobilier* (estate agent). His or her fees, usually around six per cent, will already be included in the property price, and will cover showing you various properties, finding out about annual running costs, the *taxes foncières* and *taxes d'habitation* (the annual local taxes) and making

The warm, stone Provençal architecture, the charm of the area's beaches, its enviable climate and easy-going lifestyle have encouraged many expatriates to settle here

appointments with a local *notaire* (notary), who will draw up and oversee the sale contract, and should undertake the basic searches. The notary's fee is between 6–10 per cent of the purchase cost (there is a prescribed sliding scale), and is paid over and above the purchase price.

The usual procedure is to make an offer for a property, and then, on acceptance by the vendor, pay the notary while signing a *compromis de vente*. A statutory period of time follows – usually six weeks – in which financing is organised and searches are undertaken before the finalisation of the purchase, the *acte de vente*, again requiring a signature before the notary.

Before rushing into a purchase, it is worth spending time in the area during the worst months of the year – even life in Provence is not always a bed of roses. Likewise, it is a good idea to overhaul one's linguistic skills – it is hard to make friends with the neighbours if all you can do is nod and smile. And dealing with the EDF (electricity board), France Telecom (the phone company), Générale des Eaux (water supplier), your new local bank, the local *mairie* (town hall), not to mention architects and suppliers, requires more than a basic command of the language to satisfactorily and speedily start up the running of a new home.

Children

Children who have had a surfeit of Provence's Roman remains and medieval sites deserve a break during the holiday. Attractions range from aquaparks to zoos.

Antibes
Marineland

This is a large attraction with aquariums and displays illustrating the sealife of the Mediterranean, and much else. Attractions include performing whales and dolphins, an aqua-splash, butterfly jungle and adventure golf. If you are travelling by local train, get off at Biot.
RN7-Antibes. Located just off RN7 3km (2 miles) east of Antibes and 12km (7 miles) west of Nice. 306 avenue Mozart. Tel: 04 93 33 49 49. www.marineland.fr. Open: Sept–Dec & Feb–Jun 10am–5.30pm; Jul & Aug 10am–10.30pm. Closed: Jan. Admission charge.

Avignon
Le Parc du Soleil et du Cosmos

The theme of this park is the discovery of the universe. Stars and planets speak directly to you (in French) in an imaginatively presented and educational attraction.
Avenue Charles-de-Gaulle, 30133 Les Angles, Avignon. Tel: 04 90 25 66 82. www.parcducosmos.net. Open: guided tours only Tue–Fri & Sun. Closed: late Dec. Admission charge.

La Barben
Château de la Barben

Fully furnished château and beautiful gardens with a large zoo.
13330 La Barben, just east of Salon-de-Provence. Tel: 04 90 55 19 12. www.zoolabarben.com. Open: 10am–8pm (ticket office closed weekdays in winter noon–1.30pm). Admission charge.

Bédarrides
Oxygène Aquarium Tropical

Three hundred kinds of tropical fish are displayed in this aquarium.
Between Orange and Avignon. 30 petite route de Sorgues, 84370 Bédarrides. Tel: 04 90 33 06 87. Open: Tue–Sat 10am–noon & 2–7pm (till 6pm on Sun). Admission charge.

Châteauneuf-les-Martigues
Magicland
Wild West town with daily shows, train rides and adventure playground.
Châteauneuf-les-Martigues, north of Carry-le-Rouet, 25km (16 miles) west of the centre of Marseille on the A55. Tel: 04 42 79 86 90. Open: Mar–Jun 10am–6pm; Jul & Aug Sat & Sun daily 10am–6pm. Admission charge.

Cuges-les-Pins
OK Corral
Themed Wild West funfair. Rides and shoot-outs.
13780 Cuges-les-Pins, on the RN8 between Marseille and Toulon. Tel: 04 42 73 80 05. www.okcorral.fr. Open: Mar, Sept–Nov Sat & Sun 10am–5.30pm; Apr–Jun Wed, Sat & Sun 10am–5.30pm; Jul & Aug daily 10am–5.30pm. Admission charge.

Fréjus
Parc Zoologique Safari de Fréjus
You can explore this 20-hectare (49-acre) zoo on foot or by car.
Le Capitou, 83600 Fréjus. Tel: 04 98 11 37 37. www.zoo-frejus.com. Open: Nov–Feb daily 10.30am–4.30pm; Mar–May & Sept–Oct daily 10am–5pm; Jun–Aug daily 10am–6pm. Admission charge.

Port-Cros
Sentier Sous-marin
A discovery trail for snorkellers.
Port-Cros National Park, île de Port-Cros. Tel: 04 94 01 40 70. Open: Jul & Aug daily. Admission charge.

St-Cannat
Le Village des Automates
Theme park with animated puppets.
13760 St-Cannat, between Salon-de-Provence and Aix-en-Provence. Tel: 04 42 57 30 30. Open: Apr–Sept daily 10am–6pm; Oct–Mar Wed, Sat & Sun 10am–5pm. Admission charge.

St-Tropez
Maison des Papillons
A collection of over 20,000 specimens of nocturnal butterflies and moths.
9 rue Etienne Berny, St-Tropez. Tel: 04 94 97 63 45. Open: Jun–Aug Wed–Mon 10am–noon & 2–7pm; Sept–May Wed–Mon 10am–noon & 2–6pm. Admission charge.

Sanary
Jardin Exotique Zoo
A zoo with a good bird collection.
Just north of exit 12 on motorway, Bandol. Tel: 04 94 29 40 38. www.zoosanary.com. Open: daily 8am–noon & 2–7pm (till dusk in winter). Closed: Sun afternoon. Admission charge.

Septèmes-les-Vallons
Aquacity
Huge aquapark with an amazing variety of slides.
13240 Septèmes-les-Vallons, off A51 autoroute between Marseille and Aix-en-Provence. Tel: 08 26 10 12 88. www.aquacity.fr. Open: Jun–Sept daily 10am–6pm. Admission charge.

Sport and leisure

The Provençals are no different from the rest of us in their passion for le foot (football), motor racing, tennis, golf and water sports. What sets them apart is their love of boules, cycling and bullfighting. Any gravelly patch of land is likely to be commandeered as a boules pitch for a game that seems like an impromptu version of bowls. Nowhere near as incomprehensible as cricket or American football, it is a restful game to watch, drink in hand, from the comfort of a pavement café.

Cycling is a serious, and strenuous, business in Provence. The steeper the hill, the greater the challenge – and that is quite apart from the heat. The classic cycle climb is the ascent of Mont Ventoux (a regular leg of the **Tour de France**), an energy-sapping grind of around 20km (12 miles) to an altitude of nearly 2,000m (6,562ft). The Provençal predilection for bullfighting is concentrated in the south, around the Camargue. Animal-lovers can at least rejoice in the fact the bull survives in the Provençal version.

Bullfighting

Bulls come off rather better in Provence than in Spain. The usual spectacle involves the bullfighter, or *razeteurs*, in unfixing a cockade attached to the bull's horns without hurting the animal. But before you attend a bullfight, make sure that it is not the Spanish-style *mise-à-mort* encounter.

The *arènes* (Roman amphitheatres) at Arles and Nîmes are leading venues for bullfighting (*Arles tel: 08 91 70 03 70. www.arenes-arles.com; Nîmes tel: 08 91 70 14 01. www.arenesdenimes.com*).

Cycling

Not all of Provence is for macho, masochistic cyclists. Bring your own bicycle, or hire one locally, and enjoy the flattish lands along the Rhône Valley or the Camargue. Along the coast in summer, the sheer volume of traffic can make cycling unpleasant, though you'll at least have the last laugh when it comes to parking.

Golf

The Fédération Française de Golf (*68 rue Anatole France, 9230 Levallois-Perret. Tel: 01 41 49 77 00. www.ffg.org*) regulates the sport in France. It has become very popular in the last few years and many new courses, especially on the Côte d'Azur, have opened their doors to members and guests.

Cannes Mougins Golf Club
Mougins. Tel: 04 93 75 79 13.

Golf des Baux-de-Provence
Domaine de Mauville, Les Baux-de-Provence. Tel: 04 90 54 40 20. Email: golfbauxdeprovence@wanadoo.fr

Golfe de Cap Estérel
11km (7 miles) east of St-Raphaël. Tel: 04 94 82 55 00.

Golf de Châteaublanc (Avignon)
Morières-lès-Avignon. Tel: 04 90 33 39 08. www.golfchateaublanc.com

Golf de Digne-les-Bains
Tel: 04 92 30 58 00. www.golfdigne.com

Golf de Roquebrune (near Fréjus)
Roquebrune sur Argens.
Tel: 04 94 19 60 35. www.golf-le-roc.com

Golfe de Valescure
10km (6 miles) east of Fréjus.
Tel: 04 94 82 40 46. Email: golfdevalescure@wanadoo.fr

Monte-Carlo Golf Club
Route de Mont Agel, La Turbie.
Tel: 04 92 41 50 70.

Horseriding

Horseriding and trekking are widely available in certain parts of Provence. The Camargue, in particular, has many riding centres, which offer anything from a few hours in the saddle to a full day's trekking. All equestrian activities in relation to tourism in France come under the umbrella of the centralised **Comité National du Tourisme Équestre de la Fédération Française d'Équitation**. More than 1,200 equestrian centres are listed by the FFE.

9 boulevard MacDonald, 75019 Paris.
Tel: 01 53 26 15 50. www.ffe.com

Motor racing

Monaco is the spiritual home of **Formula One Grand Prix** racing. Although the narrow street circuit is totally unsuited to today's racing cars (overtaking is virtually impossible), the Grand Prix, held in May, is still the race of the season.

During Grand Prix weekend, the cars are not the only things to change gear. Prices in Monaco and the surrounding towns, never modest at the best of times, shift up another cog in response to the glamour-seeking jet setters and the captive audience of genuine fans.

The South of France's other main motor-racing venue is the **Circuit Paul Ricard**. *Route des Hauts du Camp, Le Castellet, 83330 Le Beausset. Tel: 04 94 98 36 66. www.circuitpaulricard.com*

Skiing

Inhabitants of the Côte d'Azur live in privileged surroundings. In winter it is quite possible to water-ski along a sunny seashore in the morning and ski on snow in the afternoon. Three major ski resorts lie within a few hours' drive of Nice: **Auron**, **Isola 2000** and **Valberg**. Despite their southern latitude, they boast excellent snow records.

A little further north, in the Alpes-de-Haute-Provence, the two major ski resorts are **Pra-Loup** and

Super-Sauze near Barcelonnette.

Auron

Range: 1,600–2,500m (5,250–8,200ft) with 120km (75 miles) of piste.
Office de Tourisme, 06660 St-Étienne-de-Tinée. Tel: 04 93 02 41 96.

Isola 2000

Range: 1,800–2,600m (5,900–8,530ft) with 112km (70 miles) of piste.
Office de Tourisme, 06420 Isola.
Tel: 04 93 23 15 15.

Pra-Loup

Range: 1,500–2,500m (4,920–8,200ft) with 160km (99 miles) of piste.
Office de Tourisme, Maison de Pra-Loup,
04400 Pra-Loup. Tel: 04 92 84 10 04.
www.praloup.com

Super-Sauze

Range: 1,400–2,400m (4,590–7,875ft) with pistes to suit all skiing abilities.
Office de Tourisme, Immeuble Le Perce-Neige, 04400 Le Sauze/Super-Sauze.
Tel: 04 92 81 05 61. www.sauze.com

Valberg

Range: 1,600–2,450m (5,250–8,040ft) with 80km (50 miles) of piste and 50km (31 miles) of cross-country ski trails.
Office de Tourisme, 06470 Valberg.
Tel: 04 93 23 24 25.

There are a number of other, smaller ski resorts and stations in Provence, including: L'Audibergue, Beuil-les-Launes, Le Boréon, La Colmiane-Valdeblore, Esteng-d'Entraunes, La Foux-d'Allos, La Gordoloasque-Belvédère, Gréolières-Les-Neiges, Jausiers-la-Frache, Mont Ventoux, Montagne de Lure, Peira-Cava, Roubion-les-Buisses, St-Auban, St-Dalmas-le-Selvage, St-Jean-Montclar, Ste-Anne-la-Condamine, Tende-Caramagne, Turini-Camp-d'Argent and Val-Pelens-St-Martin-d'Entraunes.

A selection of *01891* snow information telephone numbers operates within the UK. Some of the resorts mentioned here are part of the **Ski France** service. For further information, contact:
9 rue de Madrid, 75008 Paris. Tel: 04 47 42 23 32. www.skifrance.fr

Walking and climbing

Walking and hiking are extremely well organised in France. A network of long-distance footpaths and trails covers the whole of the country, from north to south, east to west. These marked paths are known as 'GRs' (Sentiers des Grandes Randonnées), each of which bears an identifying number.

Some of the most popular walking areas in Provence are the Luberon Hills, Massif des Maures and Mont Ventoux. These areas offer hilly terrain and – in the case of the Maures and Ventoux – a good covering of cool, green forest.

The mountains of the Alpes-de-Haute-Provence and Alpes-Maritimes provide a much more serious challenge. Walkers can spend days and weeks in this dramatic landscape – the higher parts of which remain snow-covered throughout the year – stopping overnight in remote hostels or mountain huts.

Rock climbing is a major activity in the mountains. All levels of difficulty can be tackled. Experienced climbers are particularly attracted to the **Parc National du Mercantour** (*see pp137–8*), where the ascents range from difficult to very difficult.

June to October is the best time to enjoy the high mountains. Always be well prepared and keep a watch out for the weather – it can change very quickly.

Walking information
Fédération Française de la Randonnée Pédestre
Centre d'Information, 14 rue Riquet, 75019 Paris. Tel: 01 44 89 93 93. www.ffrp.asso.fr
Nature & Tourisme
Rue Voltaire, 75011 Paris. Tel: 01 43 72 15 69.

Climbing information
Club Alpin Français
24 avenue Laumière, 75019 Paris. Tel: 01 53 72 87 00. www.ffcam.fr
Fédération Française de la Montagne et de l'Escalade
8 quai Marne, 75019 Paris. Tel: 01 40 18 75 59. www.ffme.fr

Water sports
Although conditions in the placid Mediterranean are not perfect for serious sailing and windsurfing, this does not seem to put many people off. There are marinas and harbours packed with expensive yachts all along the coast. Windsurfers can easily hire equipment at many of the local beaches and sports shops.

Diving conditions are good, though marine life has suffered along the Riviera through overfishing and pollution. Away from the coast, Provence's lakes and rivers provide excellent water sports opportunities.

Further information is available from the following national organisations:

Canoeing/rafting
Fédération Française de Canoë-Kayak
87 quai de la Marne, 94340 Joinville-le-Pont. Tel: 01 45 11 08 50. www.ffck.org

Diving
Fédération Française d'Études et des Sports Sous-Marins
24 quai de Rive-Neuve, 13284 Marseille. Tel: 04 91 33 99 31. www.ffessm.fr

Water-skiing
Fédération Française de Ski Nautique
27 rue Athènes, 75009 Paris. Tel: 01 53 20 19 19. www.ffsn.fr

The Massif des Maures is ideal for walkers

Olives

The black cypress and the silvery olive tree dominate large parts of the Provençal landscape. The mournful beauty of the cypress has inspired many a poet; the olive, a tough evergreen, serves a more practical purpose. Originally imported from Greece, it has long had a vital role in the agrarian economy of Provence.

The hardy olive

One of the principal virtues of the olive, for the canny farmers of Provence, is that it thrives in barren

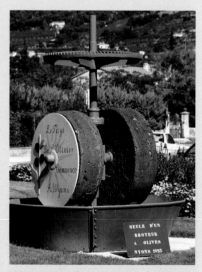

Visitors can see the entire process from growing to processing, and then buy the many varieties

areas, taking root in poor, rocky soil and surviving great heat and aridity. What is more, it is long-lived: many of the groves climbing the hillsides have been tended by successive generations of farmers. The trees grow to a height of around 7.5m (25ft) and often achieve impressive girth. Its handsome hard wood is sometimes carved into kitchen utensils and other objects.

As anyone who has visited a Provençal market will confirm, olives are taken very seriously in this part of France. For a start, there are stalls dedicated to the sale of olives and nothing else; and you are not – heaven forbid! – given a choice of merely black or green, but myriad variations on a theme, all laid out in open containers for tasting beforehand. There are olives with garlic, olives with peppers and olives with herbs, bitter and smooth-tasting olives – even plain black and green olives. The olive paste, *tapenade*, is a convenient way to bring home the taste of Provence.

Oil and cosmetics

Then there are the bottles of olive oil, a staple ingredient of Provençal culinary art. The extraction of oil from the ripened fruit is a comparatively simple process, and over the years the oil press has been as widely used in Provence as the wine press.

The olives, black when ripe, are first pressed to a pasty consistency, then put in woollen bags and subjected to considerable pressure. The resulting product is considered the finest of vegetable oils, and is used not only in food preparation but in fine soaps and cosmetics.

Provence is a well-known centre of olive production

Food and drink

Provence, like the rest of France, reveres its food. Meals are anything but a means to an end. They rise above mere sustenance into occasions with aesthetic and social dimensions – which explains why meals are never hurried, there are deliberate pauses between courses, and everything still stops for lunch.

You will always find exceptions to these generalisations, but they will be confined to the larger towns and cities where the universal fast-food mentality is making its presence felt. In small-town Provence and in the country areas, traditional values still apply. Ask the locals – they will always know the best places to eat.

Restaurants range from the very expensive (usually along the coast) to the amazingly cheap. Go for the fixed-price menu of three or four courses, with limited choice per course. Many restaurants offer a few versions of these, ranging from the basic *menu touristique* (which usually features chicken, trout, steak and chips, etc) to the elaborate *menu gastronomique* with regional specialities. Lunch menus are almost always cheaper than those for dinner. Note that last orders are around 9pm in country areas.

Bread (a cut-up *baguette*) is always provided, along with water. House wine is becoming increasingly expensive, and some of the classier bottles can be surprisingly dear in comparison to their supermarket price. If the restaurant serves local wine by the carafe or *pichet*, that will be the best value. For those with a small appetite, many cafés and bars serve snacks and light meals. Cafés will also serve breakfast – a large cup of milky coffee, bread, jam and sometimes croissants.

There are few vegetarians in France, and French restaurateurs in general do not see any need to make special allowances on their menus for customers on a strict meat- and fish-free diet. There are, however, vegetarian restaurants in Marseille, Nice and Aix-en-Provence. Everywhere else, the best options are either to choose a salad or a vegetable side dish from the menu, or to look for a foreign-run restaurant where the owners are more likely to understand vegetarian requirements.

Along with wine, the staple drink of Provence is *pastis*, a strong aniseed-flavoured aperitif served with ice and water (*see pp170–71*). Locals swear that they can tell the difference between the main brands, Pernod Anise and Ricard Pastis. Beer is served by the bottle or, in most cafés, on draught as *bière pression*, the cheaper option.

Soft drinks include *orange pressé* (freshly squeezed orange juice), *citron* (lemon) *pressé*, and fizzy Orangina. There is a wide choice of mineral waters including the famous Perrier, which is bottled locally in the west of the Rhône delta. Only ask for *café* if you like your coffee served black at paint-stripping strength. Most visitors prefer the *café crème* or *café au lait* version served with milk.

Smoking is now only allowed in outside spaces at restaurants, and in most (but by no means all) hotel rooms.

Provençal cuisine

In classic Provençal cuisine, freshness and inherent flavour are everything. Provençals leave the rich, creamy sauces to their northern countryfolk, preferring instead to let the ingredients speak for themselves.

Although garlic is liberally used, it tends to be milder in the south of France than in the north. Garlic is a mainstay of the distinctive Provençal cuisine, along with olive oil, herbs like basil, rosemary and thyme, and the tomato, or *pomme d'amour* (love apple). If you have been brought up on the bland, shrink-wrapped supermarket version of the tomato, then fear not: the plump, tasty Provençal variety is similar only in colour.

Harvest of the sea

The Provençals are justly proud of their fish dishes such as *soupe de poisson*, a work of art taking hours to prepare. A variation on this theme is the famous *bouillabaisse*, a speciality of the Marseille coast. *Bouillabaisse* is not really a soup at all. The fish are served on a side dish, while the garlic- and saffron-flavoured stew in which they were cooked comes separately so that diners can dunk their bread into it. Another classic dish is *bourride,* a white fish stew served with *aïoli*, a rich mayonnaise of garlic and olive oil known as 'the butter of Provence'.

Meat, cheese and fruit

Lamb also figures prominently in the local cuisine. The spicy *agneau de*

Breakfast overlooking the plains of western Provence

Food and drink

Tartelette au Citron

1,84 €

Delectable desserts are an integral part of Provençal cuisine

Sisteron comes from the mountain pastures of Provence, while the lambs grazing on the salt marshes of the coast provide *agneau de pré-salé*. *Boeuf à la gardianne* is a popular Camarguais beef stew cooked with red wine, vegetables, black olives and herbs. Another speciality of the region is *farci* (stuffed vegetables). Onions are stuffed with garlic, cabbages with parsley and sausage.

Cheeses, which are served before the dessert, include the local *banon*, wrapped in vine or chestnut leaves, and the peppery *poivre d'âne*. Fruit is plentiful – and be sure to make the most of the mouthwatering melons, best bought in quantity from local markets when they are just beginning to split. Vegetarians should have no trouble in finding something tempting to eat.

Eating out in Provence is a delight, and the food seems to taste even better when you dine *al fresco* on a terrace shaded by parasols or vines. Lunch is served early, from about noon, with dinner from 7–8pm. Fast food is anathema to the Provençals, and so is fast service. You are meant to take your time, and each course is served to be savoured, not rushed. *Bon appétit!*

Prices

The listing that follows is a selection of places to eat across a wide price range. The following star ratings are used to indicate the average cost per person of a three-course meal, not including drink. All taxes and service charges are usually included in the price.

★ less than €30
★★ €30–50
★★★ €50–75
★★★★ more than €75

Where to eat
Aix-en-Provence
Les Deux Garçons ★★
One of the oldest and most famous café/brasseries in France. Touristy, but it still has an original buzz and serves decent food.
53 cours Mirabeau.
Tel: 04 42 26 00 51.

La Tomate Verte ★★
A popular new place, with a modern take on Provençal cuisine.
15 rue des Tanneurs.
Tel: 04 42 60 04 58.
www.latomateverte.com

Le Clos de la Violette ★★★★
One of the top places in Aix, serving innovative

and traditional cuisine.
For best value, eat at
lunchtime on weekdays.
10 rue de la Violette.
Tel: 04 42 23 30 71.
www.closdelaviolette.com

Antibes
La Taverne du
Safranier ★–★★
In a tiny square, not far
from the Picasso
museum. Excellent fish
and seafood, often
stuffed with herbs, are
served in simple
surroundings by the
friendly owners. It has an
outside terrace.
Place du Safranier.
Tel: 04 93 34 80 50.
L'Auberge Provençale ★★
This old inn, with a
pretty garden, specialises
in fish and seafood.
61 place Nationale.
Tel: 04 93 34 13 24.
Les Vieux Murs ★★
Built into the ramparts
near the Picasso museum,
and serving Provençal
food. There is a fine view
if you sit outside.
25 Promenade Amiral
de Grasse.
Tel: 04 93 34 06 73.
Restaurant de
Bacon ★★★★
Apart from Marseille, this

is the best place to savour
bouillabaisse, the
traditional fish stew from
Provence. Also try one of
the many other delicious
seafood dishes on offer.
There is also a panoramic
view of the bay.
Boulevard de Bacon,
Cap d'Antibes.
Tel: 04 93 61 50 02. www.
restaurantdebacon.com

Arles
La Gueule de Loup ★★
Tasty local cuisine served
in a friendly atmosphere.
39 rue des Arènes.
Tel: 04 90 96 96 69.
Jardin de Manon ★★
Just a short walk from
the Roman centre, this
excellent-value restaurant
offers good Provençal
dishes with flair.
14 avenue Alyscamps.
Tel: 04 90 93 38 68.
Au Brin de
Thym ★★–★★★
Excellent, well-presented
dishes using local
produce. Tables outside
in good weather. Just off
the place du Forum.
22 rue de Docteur Fanton.
Tel: 04 90 49 95 96.
www.aubrindethym.com
Lou Marques ★★★–★★★★
The restaurant of the

hotel Jules César
provides one of the most
refined gastronomic
experiences in town.
9 boulevard des Lices.
Tel: 04 90 52 52 52.
www.hotel-julescesar.fr

Avignon
Le Moutardier du
Pape ★–★★
Directly opposite the
Palais des Papes,
particularly good value
lunch menus and
cooking of high quality.
Plenty of outside tables.
15 place du Palais.
Tel: 04 90 85 34 76.
www.restaurant-
moutardier.fr
Opéra Café ★–★★
Easily the best choice of
the many cafés in the
place de l'Horloge: good
food, good service and
good value.
24 place de l'Horloge.
Tel: 04 90 86 17 43.
La Fourchette ★★
A perennially good value,
unpretentious bistro that
serves local specialities.
17 rue Racine.
Tel: 04 90 85 20 93.
Christian Étienne ★★★★
An elegant restaurant
in fabulous
surroundings with a

Food and drink

renowned cuisine to match. One of Provence's most famous temples of gastronomy.
10 rue Mons.
Tel: 04 90 86 16 50.
www.christian-etienne.fr

Les Baux-de-Provence
Auberge de la Benvengudo ★★★★
A delightful bastide with lovely rooms and a good restaurant. Worth the short journey out of Les Baux.
Vallon de l'Arcoule, route d'Arles.
Tel: 04 90 54 32 54.
www.benvengudo.com

L'Oustau de Baumanière ★★★★
Another picturesque country house turned hotel and restaurant. Home-grown produce and a fine chef nurture a refined cuisine which is truly unique and memorable. Treat yourself, but expect to pay a big bill – it is way off the humble price scale. The nearby Cabro d'Or is under the same management, but cheaper.
Vallon de la Fontaine.

Tel: 04 90 54 33 07. www. oustaudebaumaniere.com

Beaulieu-sur-Mer
Le Max ★★
Good pizza, pasta, seafood and a large range of salads at this restaurant and bar.
Port de Plaisance.
Tel: 04 93 01 65 75.

La Reserve ★★★★
One of the finest restaurants on the coast, in this legendary hotel. Superb, surprisingly light food, smooth but friendly service and luxurious ambience.
5 boulevard du Maréchal Leclerc.
Tel: 04 93 01 00 01.
www.reservebeaulieu.com

Cannes
C Beach ★★
One of the best choices on the beach, with reasonable prices for a range of simple dishes.
Boulevard de la Croisette (opposite the Grand Hotel). Tel: 04 93 38 14 59.

Café Roma ★★
Good pasta and grills in this trendy venue with a terrace. Open late.
1 square Mérimée.
Tel: 04 93 38 05 04.

La Mère Besson ★★★–★★★★
A favourite Cannes restaurant serving authentically prepared traditional specialities.
13 rue des Frères-Pradignac.
Tel: 04 93 39 59 24.

La Palme d'Or ★★★★
The best-known gastronomic venue in Cannes – in the luxurious Martinez hotel. Chef Christian Sinicropi is highly rated for his inventive seasonal food. The hotel also has an excellent beach restaurant, ZPlage, serving (mainly) fusion food, and a casual restaurant, Le Relais – serving light dishes – by the pool. Both are much cheaper (★★–★★★) than the Palme d'Or.
73 bd de la Croisette.
Tel: 04 92 98 73 00.
www.hotel-martinez.com

Gordes
Les Bories ★★★–★★★★
Wonderful position for this good restaurant. New Provençal cuisine and a fine wine cellar.
Route de l'Abbaye de Sénanque.
Tel: 04 90 72 00 51.

L'Isle-sur-la-Sorgue
Le Bouchon ★★–★★★
On the river, and one of the best choices in town, this convivial restaurant is full of locals – with a good range of set menus serving (mostly) Provençal cuisine.
11 quai Jean-Jaurès.
Tel: 04 90 20 67 44.

Marseille
Le Pointu ★–★★
It looks unpromising, and service is slow, but here you will find some of the best food in the old port

La Colombe d'Or, St-Paul-de-Vence

area. Huge seafood salads and Provençal dishes. Outside tables.

18 cours d'Estienne d'Orves.

Tel: 04 91 55 61 53.

Chez Madie 'Les Galinettes' ★★–★★★

One of the most popular restaurants with locals in the old port. Specialises in fish fresh from the market.

138 quai du Port.

Tel: 04 91 90 40 87.

Une Table au Sud ★★★

A restaurant to note and a star chef who provides the best Provençal fare. Off the port area.

2 quai du Port.

Tel: 04 91 90 63 53.

Monaco

L'Horizon ★★–★★★

serving simpler dishes on the top floor, with great views from the terrace.

12 avenue des Spélugues.

Tel: (377) 93 50 65 00.

www.fairmont.com

Le Café de Paris ★★–★★★★

You do not have to spend a fortune here to enjoy a reasonable meal. International dishes are served in glittering *belle époque*-style

surroundings.

Place du Casino, Monte Carlo.

Tel: (377) 98 06 76 23.

L'Argentin ★★★–★★★★

Fine ingredients and flavoursome food, mainly light, in the Fairmont hotel's main restaurant. Beef is a speciality. The hotel also has a more casual restaurant.

Joël Robuchon ★★★★

Legendary chef Joël Robuchon's restaurant – with an open kitchen – at the luxurious Métropole hotel provides superb light dishes, impeccably served by friendly staff.

4 avenue de la Madone.

Tel: (377) 93 15 15 10.

www.metropole.com

Le Louis XV ★★★★

The most elegant – and still one of the best – restaurants in Monaco, located in the equally renowned Hôtel de Paris. Outstanding cuisine from Alain Ducasse served in a formal atmosphere. Very expensive but, considering the quality, worth it.

Place du Casino.

Tel: (377) 98 06 88 64.

www.alain-ducasse.com

Mougins

Le Feu Follet ★★–★★★

In a town known for expensive fine dining, this restaurant offers quality cuisine at affordable rates.

Place du commandant Lamy.

Tel: 04 93 90 15 78.

Nice

Au Long Cours ★★

A lively brasserie and pizzeria with plenty of choice (including dishes of the day) and good service. Most tables are outside.

9 cours Saleya.

Tel: 04 93 85 72 55.

L'Ane Rouge ★★★–★★★★

Small, but with a huge reputation as Nice's best seafood restaurant. Located on the harbour.

7 quai Deux-Emmanuel.

Tel: 04 93 89 49 63.

Le Chantecler ★★★★

The luxurious restaurant of the Negresco is now under Jean-Denis Rieubland (following a long line of fine chefs), and standards remain impeccably high. The hotel also has a much cheaper and more casual restaurant – La Rotonde.

37 promenade des Anglais.
Tel: 04 93 16 64 00. www.
hotel-negresco-nice.com

Nîmes
Au Flan Coco ★–★★
A good address. Small,
inexpensive and has a
friendly atmosphere.
31 rue Mûrier-d'Espagne.
Tel: 04 66 21 84 81.

Orange
Le Yaca ★–★★
Stylish setting for this
excellent restaurant.
Mediterranean-style
cuisine.
24 place Sylvain.
Tel: 04 90 34 70 03.
Le Parvis ★★–★★★
Freshly grown local
products, traditional
cooking with an original
touch and well-priced
menus explain this
restaurant's popularity.
3 cours Pourtoules.
Tel: 04 90 34 82 00.

St-Paul-de-Vence
Café de la Place ★–★★
Just by the boules pitch
at the village entrance,
this café with its terrace
and mirrored interior is a
good choice.
Place De Gaulle.
Tel: 04 93 32 80 03.

La Colombe
d'Or ★★★–★★★★
One of the most famous
spots on the coast, not
least for its superb art
collection. Yet the set
lunch is reasonably
priced for the quality of
the fairly simple food.
Place De Gaulle.
Tel: 04 93 32 80 02.
www.la-colombe-dor.com

St-Raphaël
L'Arbousier ★★–★★★
A modern ambience and
the gastronomic menu
ensure the popularity of
this excellent restaurant.
6 avenue de Valescure.
Tel: 04 94 95 25 00.
www.arbousier.net

St-Rémy-de-Provence
Café des Arts ★
A cheerful and
atmospheric local
institution serving
simple food.
30 boulevard Victor-Hugo.
Tel: 04 90 92 08 50.
La Gousse d'Ail ★★
A local favourite serving
high-quality traditional
food, with live jazz
on Wednesdays in
summer.
6 boulevard Marceau.
Tel: 04 90 92 16 87.

St-Tropez
Bistrot des Lices ★★★
Glamorous bistro that
pulls in the celebrities.
A perennial favourite.
3 place des Lices.
Tel: 04 94 97 11 33.
La Table du Marché ★★★
A popular venue for its
local specialities and
innovative, changing
menu.
38 rue Georges
Clemenceau.
Tel: 04 94 97 85 20.

Vaison-la-Romaine
Le Beffroi ★★–★★★
The views from this
16th-century hotel and
restaurant are expansive
and take in all the
medieval town.
Good menus featuring
regional cuisine.
Rue de l'Évêché,
Haute Ville.
Tel: 04 90 36 04 71.
Le Moulin à Huile ★★★
Gastronomic dining took
a turn for the better
when this restaurant
gained its Michelin star.
A fine position near the
river matches an
inventive cuisine.
1 quai du Maréchal Foch.
Tel: 04 90 36 20 67.
www.moulin-huile.com

Wines and spirits

Drinking a glass or two of a chewy, deeply textured Côtes-du-Rhône – a Cairanne perhaps, or a Gigondas, Rasteau or Vacqueyras – on the terrace on a warm summer's evening is one of the great pleasures of Provence. And it is a pleasure made even more satisfying in the knowledge that this full-bodied red wine, bought direct from the local vineyard, has cost little more than the standard supermarket plonk back home.

The reds of the Rhône

Parts of Provence are almost entirely dedicated to the production of wine: drive along the flanks of the Rhône Valley around Orange and Avignon, and you will see regimented rows of vines stretching into the distance. These vineyards yield the robust, peppery generic Côtes-du-Rhône and the even better versions named after individual villages or growers.

The top wine from the region is Châteauneuf-du-Pape, a full, rich red

Rasteau produces award-winning Côtes-du-Rhône

The region's vineyards produce some of France's most famous wines

with a perfumed raspberry bouquet, which often does not peak until a decade or so after bottling.

Although its reds reign supreme (a consequence of the hot climate), Provence produces wines to suit all occasions. In addition to the deep – and highly alcoholic – reds, there are delicate rosés and dry and sweet whites. Tavel and Lirac rosés are both exceptionally good. Beaumes-de-Venise is mostly famous for its thick, sweet wine made from the muscat grape and served chilled as an apéritif or dessert wine (a similar wine is produced in Rasteau), though some exceptional red wines are also made here.

The wines from the coastal strip around Bandol – reds, rosés and whites – have a character all their own, while the whites of nearby Cassis are fresh and aromatic.

Other, less well-known wine-producing areas in Provence include Côtes-du-Ventoux, Côtes-du-Luberon, Côtes-de-Provence and Côteaux d'Aix.

Strong stuff

Pay attention to the alcoholic content of Provençal wines. It tends to be higher – in some cases, substantially so – than the usual 10 to 12 degrees proof. The same word of warning applies to *pastis*, the traditional aniseed-flavoured spirit drink of Provence. Normally over 50 degrees proof (though you can purchase weaker versions), it is served as a long drink, and the spirit turns milky when ice and water are added.

Accommodation

For families and couples, hotels in France usually offer good value because you pay by the room, not per person. Along the Riviera, however, this money-saving arrangement is undermined by high room rates, but in rural Provence you will usually be pleasantly surprised by the accommodation you can purchase for a relatively modest sum.

Many visitors to Provence – especially families or large groups of friends – prefer to self-cater. Along the coast, and in the hills just inland, there is a large choice of apartments and luxury villas. Summer rates for the sought-after properties are high. For better value, go further inland – which, in any case, is the true Provence – and rent a more modest country property. There are many websites, and various magazines about France, where rental properties are advertised.

Camping, of course, is the ultimate budget alternative. The French are a nation of ardent campers, so you can expect to find an excellent choice of sites with comprehensive facilities.

There is a wide range of hotels to choose from in Provence and on the Côte d'Azur, from simple, family-run places to among the most glamorous hotels in the world. A good view, particularly of the sea, will always cost you considerably more. So – if that doesn't matter to you, or your budget is limited – choose a place slightly away from the main attractions. Also, make sure that breakfast is included when you book, otherwise the cost can be an unpleasant surprise – although an alternative, if you are in a town, is simply to go to a local café for a continental breakfast. Many hotels are closed out of season. However, if you choose to go in the low season you will find that prices – particularly on the coast – can be quite reasonable; and remember that the weather can often be good in spring and autumn. Note that prices normally rise during major local events.

Prices

The following star ratings are used to indicate the average cost per double room, including breakfast. All taxes and service charges are usually included in the price.

★	less than €100
★★	€100–200
★★★	€200–300
★★★★	more than €300

Aix-en-Provence

Des Augustins ★★
In an old convent off the cours Mirabeau. No restaurant, but comfortable rooms. You can have breakfast in the garden.
3 rue de Masse.
Tel: 04 42 27 28 59.
www.hotel-augustins.com

Le Pigonnet ★★★–★★★★
One of the best hotels in Aix, with a lovely garden, a pool, excellent restaurant, well-decorated rooms and good service. The hotel generally has a relaxing and stylish ambience – and it is well located, near many of the main sights.
5 avenue du Pigonnet.
Tel: 04 42 59 02 90.
www.hotelpigonnet.com

Antibes

La Jabotte ★–★★
A pleasant small hotel, recently redecorated, with rooms opening on to a central courtyard, where you can have breakfast.
13 avenue Max Maurey, Cap d'Antibes.
Tel: 04 93 61 45 89.
www.jabotte.com

La Place ★–★★
A newly refurbished small hotel with a restaurant. The quality of rooms is far more stylish than you might expect for the price.
1 avenue du 24 août.
Tel: 04 97 21 03 11.
www.la-place-hotel.com

Cap d'Antibes Beach Hotel ★★★★
Opened in 2009, this small, stylish, modern hotel (a short walk from Juan-les-Pins) has a fine gastronomic restaurant, Les Pêcheurs, its own private beach (with a good restaurant), a swimming pool, parking and a small spa. There is a choice of sea view and garden rooms, all with their own balcony or terrace.
10 boulevard Maréchal Juin. Tel: 04 92 93 13 30.
www.ca-beachhotel.com

Arles

L'Arlatan ★★–★★★
In a fine 15th–17th-century building, off the place du Forum, with an outside courtyard, a pool, and some rooms with private terraces. Traditional décor.

26 rue Sauvage. Tel: 04 90 93 56 66. www.hotel-arlatan.fr

Jules César ★★★–★★★★
A fine hotel in an old convent, with traditional Provençal furnishings. It has a huge lobby, a top-class restaurant, a courtyard with a lovely garden, and a pool. For many, the best address in Arles. Given its location, it is also surprisingly peaceful.
9 boulevard des Lices.
Tel: 04 92 52 52 52.
www.hotel-julescesar.fr

Nord Pinus ★★★/★★★★
One-time home-from-home to artists such as Picasso and Cocteau, as well as many bullfighters (as the décor demonstrates) this hotel is about the most fashionable in Arles. Its old-world brasserie still pulls in the crowds for its excellent and innovative cuisine.
Place du Forum.
Tel: 04 90 93 44 44.
www.nord-pinus.com

Avignon

De Garlande ★–★★
A simple hotel converted from two old houses.

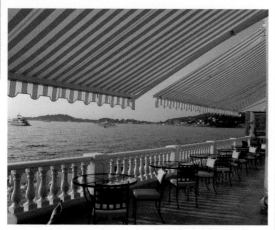

La Réserve has superb views over the Mediterranean

Well located for the main sights.
20 rue Garlande. Tel: 04 90 80 08 85.
www.hoteldegarlande.com

Cloître Saint Louis ★★–★★★
The main building, originally a Jesuit seminary (with a lovely chapel) dates from the late 16th century. The modern extension was designed by leading architect Jean Nouvel. The hotel has a rooftop swimming pool and a restaurant.
20 rue du Portail Boquier. Tel: 04 90 27 55 55. www. cloitre-saint-louis.com

Auberge de Cassagne ★★★–★★★★
On the outskirts of Avignon, this is a very good choice, if you're driving. A highly regarded gastronomic restaurant, restful gardens, a pool, a spa and most rooms (all very comfortable, and well appointed) with private terrace. Food and drink prices, however, are high.
430 allée de Cassagne. Tel: 04 90 31 04 18. www. aubergedecassagne.com

La Mirande ★★★★
Just by the Palais des Papes, very stylishly decorated, with a courtyard, a good restaurant and a calm ambience.
4 place de l'Amirante. Tel: 04 90 14 20 20. www.la-mirande.fr

Beaulieu-sur-Mer
Frisia ★–★★
Just above the yacht harbour, with sea views from many rooms (with balconies), this well-kept, comfortable hotel (with a bar and a terrace) is a good value choice, particularly given its location.
2 boulevard Eugène Gauthier.
Tel: 04 93 01 01 04.
www.frisia-beaulieu.com

La Réserve ★★★★
If it's elegance, luxury and superb, discreet (but friendly) service you're after, this is the place to come. Add in a restaurant with two Michelin stars, the spa and the magnificent views – not only from the large pool and the breakfast terrace, but also from most rooms – and you have an unbeatable combination which has appealed to many famous personalities over the years. With only 39 rooms, the hotel is also pleasantly peaceful and intimate.
5 boulevard du Maréchal Leclerc.

Tel: 04 93 01 00 01.
www.reservebeaulieu.com

Cannes
Oxford ★–★★
A ten-minute walk from the Croisette, this small, family-run hotel, recently renovated, has a garden/terrace and parking.
148 boulevard de la République.
Tel: 04 93 68 40 83.
www.oxfordhotel.fr

Villa Tosca ★–★★
Comfortable, decent room facilities (though most rooms only have showers) and well located.
11 rue Hoche.
Tel: 04 93 38 34 40.
www.villa-tosca.com

Splendid ★★
Near the old port and the Palais des Festivals. Many rooms in this pleasant hotel have balconies and views of the port.
4 rue Félix Faure.
Tel 04 97 06 22 22. www.splendid-hotel-cannes.fr

Cézanne ★★–★★★
A comfortable, modern, well-located boutique hotel with a garden, a fitness room and a small spa. A big attraction is its private beach (with restaurant), C Beach, a ten-minute walk away. It has a sister hotel, the Renoir.
40 boulevard d'Alsace.
Tel: 04 92 59 41 00.
www.hotel-cezanne.com

Martinez ★★★★
One of the great seaside hotels, this Art Deco building, dating from 1929, has everything you could need: great service, a splendid new spa, a pool, as well as sea views from many of its spacious rooms. It also has the best restaurant in Cannes (the Palme d'Or), a private beach (with the YPlage restaurant), a casual restaurant where you can have breakfast, and a lively bar.
73 boulevard de la Croisette.
Tel: 04 92 98 73 00.
www.hotel-martinez.com

Marseille
Grand Hôtel Beauvau ★★–★★★
Recently upgraded to a high standard, with great views of the Vieux Port. It has a bar, though no restaurant and few leisure facilities. But it is very well located.
4 rue Beauvau.
Tel: 04 91 54 91 00.
www.accorhotels.com

Radisson SAS ★★–★★★
A new hotel on the Vieux Port with very well-equipped rooms, a restaurant, café, fitness centre, pool and bar.
38–40 quai de Rive Neuve. Tel: 04 88 92 19 50.
www.radissonblu.com

Menton
Narev's ★
A simple, basic hotel located in a pedestrianised area of the old town. A good budget choice. No restaurant.
12 bis rue Loredan-Larchey. Tel: 04 93 35 21 31. www.hotel-narevs.com

Chambord ★–★★
A garden, but no restaurant. Centrally located and good value.
6 avenue Boyer.
Tel: 04 93 35 94 19.
www.hotel-chambord.com

Riva ★★
Good facilities and many rooms with sea views.
600 promenade du Soleil.
Tel: 04 92 10 92 10.
www.rivahotel.com

Monaco

Columbus ★★–★★★

In the Fontvieille area of Monaco, this chic, modern hotel, part-owned by racing driver David Coulthard, has a pool, a brasserie (with terrace), a gym and a cocktail bar.

23 avenue des Papalins. Tel: (377) 92 05 90 00. www.columbushotels.com

Novotel Monte-Carlo ★★–★★★

Opened in 2008 in a former radio station, central, and very well appointed for the price. It has a pool and a good restaurant. Many of the impressively designed rooms have balconies and harbour views.

16 boulevard de Princesse Charlotte. Tel: (377) 99 99 83 00. www.accorhotels.com

Fairmont ★★★★

Very high standards of service and comfort for such a big hotel. All the rooms have recently been modernised, and have balconies, many with great sea views. The food is good, too, whether you have dinner at L'Argentin or a more casual lunch or dinner outdoors on the terrace of L'Horizon. Rather like a cruise liner, it's almost a resort in itself. Its many facilities include a large heated rooftop pool, shops, a casino and a brand-new spa offering top-quality treatments. The Saphir bar is open 24 hours.

12 avenue des Spélugues. Tel: (377) 93 50 65 00. www.fairmont.com

Metropole ★★★★

With strong claims to be the best hotel in town, it offers quiet luxury, attentive service, excellent breakfasts, and two restaurants, one of them Japanese (both under the direction of Joël Robuchon), of the highest quality. If it's pampering you want, the ESPA spa is another attraction.

4 avenue de la Madone. Tel: (377) 93 15 15 15. www.metropole.com

Nice

Villa La Tour ★–★★

The only hotel in Nice's old town. Simple, but unusually good for the price. It has a roof terrace.

4 rue de la Tour. Tel: 04 93 80 08. www.villa-la-tour.com

Windsor ★★–★★★

One of the most unconventional hotels in Nice, with rooms designed by local artists. It has a peaceful garden and reliable food.

11 rue Dalpozzo. Tel: 04 93 88 59 35. www. hotelwindsornice.com

Hi Hotel ★★★

If ever there was a 'design' hotel, this is it. It has a roof terrace with a small pool and a private beach. Very popular, but not for everyone.

3 avenue des Fleurs. Tel: 04 97 07 26 26. www.hi-hotel.net

Negresco ★★★★

A local landmark, with a guest list to die for. The décor is a little camp for some, but it remains the best hotel in Nice, amply enhanced by its private beach and fine restaurant.

37 promenade des Anglais. Tel: 04 93 16 64 00. www. hotel-negresco-nice.com

Nîmes

Royal ★–★★

A good budget choice, centrally located, with a

restaurant and bar.
*3 boulevard Alphonse
Daudet. Tel 04 66 58 28
27. www.royalhotel-
nimes.com*
Novotel Atria ★★–★★★
Good facilities (including
parking – for a fee) in
this modern hotel near
the Roman arena.
*5 boulevard de Prague.
Tel: 04 66 76 56 56.
www.novotel.com*

St-Jean-Cap-Ferrat
Royal Riviera ★★★★
Pleasantly casual for a
luxury hotel, and
popular with families.
You can have lunch at
the pool bar/restaurant,
or a meal on the more
formal terrace. There are

also beauty and fitness
facilities, a large pool,
and a small beach – a
rarity in the area.
Though it's not cheap,
prices are lower than for
many other hotels of this
standard in the area.
*3 avenue Jean Monnet.
Tel: 04 93 76 31 00.
www.royal-riviera.com*

St-Paul-de-Vence
**La Colombe d'Or
★★★–★★★★**
Even though it has an
amazing guest list of
movie stars, rock royalty
and artists (many of
whom contributed their
work – which you can
see throughout the hotel
– in return for food and

lodging), this remains
a fairly simple hotel,
with a good restaurant
and a pool.
*Place De Gaulle. Tel: 04
93 32 80 02. www.la-
colombe-dor.com*

St-Tropez
Le Sube ★–★★★
The only hotel on the
port, good value for the
location and a friendly
atmosphere. Small
rooms, but some
have a view. The bar
is a lively local
meeting point.
*15 quai Suffren.
Tel: 04 94 97 30 04.*
Le Yaca ★★★/★★★★
A hotel with character, in
the centre of town. It has
well appointed rooms, a
restaurant and a pool.
*1 boulevard d'Aumale.
Tel: 04 94 55 81 00.
www.hotel-le-yaca.fr*

Villefranche-sur-Mer
Welcome ★★–★★★
Right on the harbour,
with smallish but
attractive rooms.
Certainly the best place
to stay in Villefranche.
*3 quai Amiral Courbet.
Tel: 04 93 76 27 62.
www.welcomehotel.com*

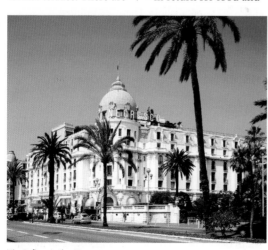

Nice's finest, the Negresco

Practical guide

Arriving

By car

With the ease of access to the Continent and the excellent motorway system in France, many visitors choose to drive to Provence or the Côte d'Azur. The most popular cross-Channel route is now **Le Shuttle**, the Eurotunnel (*tel: 0870 535 3535; www.eurotunnel.com*) train route leaving from near Folkestone to Calais/Coquelles with up to four departures per hour during peak times and a crossing time of just 35 minutes. Alternatively, the ferries from Dover to Calais (**P&O**, UK *tel: 0870 598 0333;* France *tel: 08 25 12 01 56; www.poferries.com* and **Seafrance**, *tel: 08704 431 653; www.seafrance.com*) are a more leisurely way to cross the Channel. For a longer crossing, the ferry services run from Portsmouth to St-Malo, Cherbourg, Caen and Le Havre (contact **Brittany Ferries**, *tel: 0870 366 9765; www.brittany-ferries.com* or P&O for details of their crossings); and from Newhaven to Dieppe (contact P&O for details of their crossings).

Visitors who want to travel by train with their car can board at Calais and alight in Avignon or Nice (for information, contact **Motorail** bookings, *tel: 0870 241 5415; www.raileurope.co.uk* and **Rail Savers**, *tel: 0870 750 7070; www.railsavers.com*).

From Calais, there is the autoroute (motorway) all the way to the south of France (Calais to Nice is around 1,220km/758 miles, depending on your route, and takes around 11 hours to drive). It is the fastest way to arrive in the south of the country, and although the tolls are quite expensive, and the route often congested at holiday times (avoid Saturday travel in peak season at all cost), it is still the best option.

The easiest route from Calais is to avoid the congestion of Paris's *périphérique* ring road, and to take the A26/A5/A31 route, rejoining the A6 north of Dijon.

If you prefer to drive at a more leisurely pace, taking a few days to reach Provence, then use the excellent toll-free system of well-maintained and marked N (national) and D (departmental) roads. As you drive along these less travelled routes, you will get a real taste of the country as a whole. There are numerous *gîtes* and hotels (*see pp172–7*) along the way. A useful site for gauging driving conditions is *www.bison-fute.equipement.gouv.fr*

By train

Rail passengers without a car will find that the **SNCF**'s (*www.sncf.fr*) excellent TGV (Train à Grande Vitesse) services are the fastest way to reach Avignon, Aix-en-Provence, Marseille, St-Raphaël or Nice. If combining this with a ticket on the **Eurostar** (*www.eurostar.com*) from London (St Pancras), a change in train will be necessary either in Paris or

Lille. For travel on the intercity (Grandes Lignes) or regional (TER) trains, as well as Eurostar, a range of tickets and rail passes at advantageous tariffs can be bought through the **Rail Shop** (Rail Europe Travel Centre, 1 Regent Street, London SW1Y 4XT; *tel: 0844 848 4070; www.raileurope.co.uk*).

By coach

National Express Eurolines are a budget alternative to rail travel. Coaches operate direct on a number of routes including six weekly summer schedule services to Avignon and Nîmes, while destinations on the Côte d'Azur are served three times a week with a change of coach in Lyons. For full details contact **National Express** (*tel: 08705 808 080; www.nationalexpress.com*).

By air

Provence and the Côte d'Azur are well served by scheduled flights to several airports: Nice-Côte d'Azur (*tel: 08 20 42 33 33*), Marseille-Provence (*tel: 04 42 14 14 14*) and Nîmes-Arles-Camargue (*tel: 04 66 70 49 49*). Lyon-St-Exupéry (*tel: 08 26 80 08 26*) is worth considering, since the autoroute links from Lyons to the rest of the region make it a convenient gateway. Ryanair also flies to Toulon-Hyères and Flybe to Avignon. And in 2009 Aer Lingus started flights (at very competitive fares) from Gatwick to Nice in summer.

Airlines flying to the area include:
Aer Lingus (*www.aerlingus.com*).
Air France (*www.airfrance.com*).

British Airways (*www.britishairways.com*).
British Midland (*www.flybmi.com*, or *www.bmibaby.com*).
easyJet (*www.easyjet.com*).
flybe (*www.flybe.com*).
Ryanair (*www.ryanair.com*).

Climate

Provence, which consists of high mountains as well as a Mediterranean coastline, has some regional variations in its climate; for example, the ferocious wind known as the *mistral* (*see p7*) affects mainly the Rhône Valley. Nevertheless, overall Provence is a sunny place.

June and September are the best months to travel. The weather is pleasantly hot (and can remain so into October), the days are long, and there

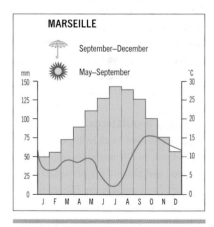

WEATHER CONVERSION CHART

25.4mm = 1 inch
°F = 1.8 × °C + 32

are no summer crowds. It can become very hot in July and August.

It does not rain very often in Provence – but when it does, it pours. Late August and September can bring torrential downpours. Average rainfall, though, is low, less than 800mm (31 inches) a year. If Provence has a rainy season, then it is in November and December.

Conversion tables

Clothes (except for women's dresses) and shoes sizes follow the standard sizes for the 'Rest of Europe'. *See tables opposite.*

Crime

Car theft is particularly rife in the Camargue and some of the main cities, so be careful where you park your car and make sure that all valuables are locked away safely out of sight. Wear a moneybelt, or keep your bag strapped across your body. If you are robbed, contact the police immediately and get a signed note for your insurance claim (*déclaration de perte*). *See also* Emergency telephone numbers, *p182.*

Customs regulations

EU citizens over 18 may import or export reasonable amounts of perfume, tobacco and alcohol for personal use. Visitors from outside the EU are bound by the following restrictions: 400 cigarettes, 100 cigarillos, 50 cigars or 250g tobacco, 60cc perfume, 2 litres still table wine, 250cc eau de toilette and 1 litre spirits or strong liqueurs over 22 per cent volume or 2 litres

fortified wine sparkling wine or other liqueurs.

Driving

In France you drive on the right. Although generalisation is a tricky business, it is fair to say that the French tend to drive faster – and are more impetuous – than Britons or Americans.

Accidents

If no police are around, note the number of the other vehicle involved, lock your car and go with the driver of the other vehicle in search of a police officer, who will make out a report in triplicate. Try to obtain names and addresses of witnesses. Send the report to your insurance company. If the accident is serious, take photos.

Breakdowns

If your car does not have hazard warning lights, you must carry a warning triangle, which you should place 30m (98ft) behind your car in the event of a breakdown. You must carry a set of spare headlight bulbs. On autoroutes there are emergency telephones every 2km ($1^1/4$ miles).

Car hire

To hire a car in France, drivers must have been in possession of a valid driving licence for at least one year. The minimum age for renting is 20, though some companies insist on 25.

Car rental is easily available throughout Provence, but it is more expensive than in most other European countries. Ask at your travel agent for details of fly-drive holidays; it is usually much cheaper to book your car and flight this way than separately.

All the major car hire companies are represented at airports and cities in Provence. If you make your reservation before your departure, you may be able to take advantage of discounts.

Documents

You will need to bring your driving licence, the vehicle registration document and insurance certificate. Although a Green Card – which gives you comprehensive cover and is available from your insurance company – is no longer required by law, it is strongly recommended.

Petrol

Please bear in mind that in some of Provence's remoter country areas, petrol stations are few, and may well be closed on Sundays. Look out for cheaper prices at larger supermarkets and hypermarkets.

Rules of the road

The *priorité à droite* (priority to the right) rule still causes confusion. Outside built-up areas, traffic flowing on the main route usually has the right of way at junctions and crossroads, which are normally signposted with a cross saying *Passage Protégé*. Within built-up areas, vehicles coming from the right – even on the

Practical guide

CONVERSION TABLE

FROM	TO	MULTIPLY BY
Inches	Centimetres	2.54
Feet	Metres	0.3048
Yards	Metres	0.9144
Miles	Kilometres	1.6090
Acres	Hectares	0.4047
Gallons	Litres	4.5460
Ounces	Grams	28.35
Pounds	Grams	453.6
Pounds	Kilograms	0.4536
Tons	Tonnes	1.0160

To convert back, for example from centimetres to inches, divide by the number in the third column.

MEN'S SUITS

UK	36	38	40	42	44	46	48
Rest of Europe	46	48	50	52	54	56	58
USA	36	38	40	42	44	46	48

DRESS SIZES

UK	8	10	12	14	16	18
France	36	38	40	42	44	46
Italy	38	40	42	44	46	48
Rest of Europe	34	36	38	40	42	44
USA	6	8	10	12	14	16

MEN'S SHIRTS

UK	14	14.5	15	15.5	16	16.5	17
Rest of Europe	36	37	38	39/40	41	42	43
USA	14	14.5	15	15.5	16	16.5	17

MEN'S SHOES

UK	7	7.5	8.5	9.5	10.5	11
Rest of Europe	41	42	43	44	45	46
USA	8	8.5	9.5	10.5	11.5	12

WOMEN'S SHOES

UK	4.5	5	5.5	6	6.5	7
Rest of Europe	38	38	39	39	40	41
USA	6	6.5	7	7.5	8	8.5

most minor roads – still have priority. In practice, the French seem as confused as the rest of us over the interpretation of this arcane rule – so be extra-vigilant at junctions and, if in doubt, give way.

In recent years, the French have discovered the value of roundabouts – new ones have cropped up all over the country. Thankfully, an unambiguous rule applies: you must give way to vehicles already on the roundabout, as instructed by the sign *Vous n'avez pas la priorité* (you do not have priority).

In addition to a warning triangle and headlight bulbs, your car should have a national identity sticker and be fitted with headlight beam deflectors. Under-10s should travel in the rear seats, and the wearing of all seat belts fitted in the car is compulsory.

Speed limits

Speeds in brackets relate to adverse weather conditions (heavy rain, fog, ice, etc).
Toll motorways: 130km/h/80mph (110km/h/68mph).
Non-toll motorways and dual carriageways: 110km/h/68mph (100km/h/62mph).
Other roads: 90km/h/55mph (80km/h/50mph).
Towns and built-up areas: 50km/h/31mph.

Please note: *Rappel* means the continuation of a restriction or of a previously signposted speed limit.

The minimum speed for the outside lane of a motorway during daylight on level ground with good visibility is 80km/h/50mph.

Electricity

The supply is 220 volts using continental two-pin round plugs. Remember to pack an adaptor.

Embassies and consulates

Australia
4 rue Jean-Rey, 75724 Paris, Cedex 15. Tel: 01 40 59 33 00.

Canada
35 avenue Montaigne, 75008 Paris. Tel: 01 44 43 29 00.

Ireland
4 rue Rude, 75016 Paris. Tel: 01 44 17 67 00.

New Zealand
7 rue Léonard-da-Vinci, 75016 Paris. Tel: 01 45 01 43 43.

UK
35 rue du Faubourg St-Honoré, 75383 Paris, Cedex 08. Tel: 01 44 51 31 00. Consular section: 18 bis rue d'Anjou, 75008 Paris. Tel: 01 44 51 31 01. Also at 24 avenue du Prado, 13006 Marseille. Tel: 04 91 15 72 10.

USA
2 avenue Gabriel, 75382 Paris, Cedex 08. Tel: 01 43 12 22 22. Also at Place Varian Fry, 13086 Marseille. Tel: 04 91 54 92 00.

Emergency telephone numbers

Ambulance *15*   **Fire** *18*
Police *17*   **Emergencies** *112*

Health

There are no mandatory vaccination requirements, and no vaccination recommendations other than to keep tetanus and polio immunisation up to date. As in every other part of the world, AIDS is present. It is quite safe to drink the tap water served in hotels and restaurants, but never drink from a tap labelled *eau non potable* (not drinking water).

Hitchhiking

In Provence, unlike other parts of France, hitchhiking is quite common. The usual common-sense provisos apply, however; do not hitchhike alone, and be wary of isolated spots. Hitchhiking is not allowed on autoroutes.

Insurance

All EU countries have reciprocal arrangements for reclaiming the cost of medical services. Under an EU reciprocal arrangement, visitors from EU countries are entitled to medical treatment in France, but should obtain a European Health Insurance Card from their own National Social Security office or from post offices in the UK. This should be presented to the doctor if possible before treatment or a consultation starts. Claiming is often a long-drawn-out process, and you are only covered for medical care, not for emergency repatriation, holiday cancellation and so on. You are strongly advised to take out a travel insurance policy from your own insurance company or a travel agent.

Lost property

Report loss of valuables to the police and get a copy of the statement for making an insurance claim. Cancel lost credit cards and traveller's cheques immediately. A lost passport should be reported at once to your nearest embassy or consulate.

Media

In most of the major towns and cities, English-language newspapers are widely available. *Le Monde* is a respected national daily newspaper. To look up listings and local events the regional newspapers such as *La Marseillaise* or *Nice-Matin*, the leftist *Le Provençal* and the right-wing *Le Méridional* are more informative. Along the Côte d'Azur you will be able to pick up the English-language *Riviera Reporter*.

Money matters

The unit of currency is the euro, which is made up of 100 cents. Bank hours vary, but typical times are Monday to Friday, 9am–noon, 2–4pm. All banks are closed on Sunday and public holidays. Some open on Saturday but close on Monday.

ATMs are now commonplace in cities, towns and larger villages, and the exchange rate tends to be better than at bureaux de change. Remember to take your PIN, and check what charges your bank will levy on withdrawals.

A useful means of paying is a currency card, which you load up with euros online, and then use as you would a credit card. The advantage is that you know exactly the rate you are paying: the rate at which you bought your euros. The best deals are at *www.fairfx.com* and *www.caxtonfx.com*

Opening hours

Apart from the big cities, Provence shuts down between noon and 2pm or later every day. In compensation, shops open very early, and many – especially the smaller stores – do not close until quite late, sometimes 8pm.

Many petrol stations and the larger supermarkets remain open throughout the day, especially in summer, as do tourist attractions and tourist offices.

Normal business hours are 8/9am–noon, and 2–6pm. Note that public holidays are taken very seriously in France and that banks, post offices, public buildings, many shops and most museums will be closed. Public transport timetables are also affected. So always check.

Pharmacies

Pharmacies, recognised by the sign of a green cross, provide medical advice and sell a wide range of products (prescription and non-prescription). Many stock familiar brands of nappies (*couches*), tampons and sanitary towels (*serviettes hygiéniques*), though these can also be bought at supermarkets. Machines dispensing condoms

(*préservatifs*) are often installed outside pharmacies. You will always find an open pharmacy in the area – details are posted on pharmacy doors.

Places of worship

Every town and village has a Catholic church. There are synagogues in Avignon, Carpentras and Cavaillon; Protestant churches in Nice, Toulon, Aix, Marseille and Avignon, and mosques in Marseille, Nice and Toulon.

Police

Country areas and smaller places are covered by the Gendarmerie police force (blue trousers, black jackets and white belts). In towns and cities, policing is provided by the Police Municipale (blue uniforms). The highway police are the Garde Mobile or Police de la Route. The emergency telephone number is *17*. In the case of very serious problems, you should contact your Consulate.

Post offices

The post office is known as *La Poste* – branches are usually open 9am–noon and 2–5pm, though there are many variations. You can buy stamps or telephone cards here, and some will change Euro-cheques. If you just want stamps, you can purchase them at *tabacs* (tobacconists) and some hotels.

You can use post offices to receive mail through the poste restante system. Letters should be addressed with your surname printed in capital letters and

Language

Even if you speak only a little French, the effort will be appreciated. English is widely spoken on the coast, much less so in rural Provence. But whatever your location, you will find that your attempts to speak French, however limited, will go down well.

yes	oui	**petrol**	l'essence
no	non	**airline**	la ligne aérienne
please	s'il vous plaît	**Do you speak English?**	Parlez-vous anglais?
(any request or enquiry should be accompanied by this phrase)		**I do not understand**	Je ne comprends pas
		OK/agreed	D'accord
thank you	merci	**Where?**	Où?
good day/	bonjour	**How much?/**	Combien?
good morning		**How many?**	
(when addressing anyone in this way, it is common courtesy to add *monsieur* for a man, *madame* for a woman or *mademoiselle* for a girl or young woman)		**Excuse me**	Pardon
		Have you a room?	Avez-vous une chambre?
		Have you a room with a private bath?	Avez-vous une chambre avec bain?
		How much does it cost?	Combien ça coûte?
good evening	bonsoir	**I feel ill**	Je suis malade
goodbye	au revoir	**Have you a double room?**	Avez-vous une chambre lit double?
yesterday	hier		
today	aujourd'hui		
tomorrow	demain		
the morning	le matin		
afternoon	l'après-midi	**0**	zéro
the evening	le soir	**1**	un, une
man	un homme	**2**	deux
woman	une femme	**3**	trois
big	grand	**4**	quatre
small	petit	**5**	cinq
a lot	beaucoup	**6**	six
a little	un peu	**7**	sept
open	ouvert	**8**	huit
closed	fermé	**9**	neuf
hot	chaud	**10**	dix
cold	froid	**11**	onze
car	une voiture	**12**	douze
railway station	la gare	**13**	treize
bus station	la gare routière	**14**	quatorze
bakery	une boulangerie	**15**	quinze
supermarket	un supermarché	**16**	seize
bank	une banque	**17**	dix-sept
toilets	les toilettes	**18**	dix-huit
post office	la poste	**19**	dix-neuf
stamp	un timbre	**20**	vingt
chemist	la pharmacie	**21**	vingt et un
hospital	l'hôpital		

22	vingt-deux
30	trente
40	quarante
50	cinquante
60	soixante
70	soixante-dix
80	quatre-vingts
90	quatre-vingt-dix
100	cent
200	deux cents
300	trois cents
1,000	mille
2,000	deux mille
1,000,000	un million

Monday	lundi
Tuesday	mardi
Wednesday	mercredi
Thursday	jeudi
Friday	vendredi
Saturday	samedi
Sunday	dimanche

underlined, followed by Poste Restante, Poste Centrale, and the postcode and name of the town.

Public transport

Along the main communication corridors in Provence – the north-south Rhône Valley and the east-west Côte d'Azur – rail and bus services are very good. Buses and trains also operate in rural and mountainous Provence, but services are patchy.

For details of up-to-date rail services and ferries from Marseille and Nice, consult the bi-monthly publication *Thomas Cook European Rail Timetable*. This is available to buy online at *www.thomascookpublishing.com* or from Thomas Cook offices (*tel: 01733 416477*).

By bus

In addition to the main rail routes, a line runs up the Durance Valley into the Alps. There are many local bus companies but not much coordination of services. There are also local buses run by SNCF (French Railways), which serve places on rail routes where trains do not stop (rail tickets and passes are valid on these).

The only feasible way to explore off-the-beaten-track Provence is by car, bicycle or on foot. Local tourist offices and bus stations are good sources of advice and information.

By rail

For details of unlimited-travel rail passes, contact:

In UK The Rail Shop, *1 Regent Street, London SW1Y 4XT. Tel: 0844 848 4070 for train information. www.raileurope.co.uk*
In USA Rail Europe, *44 South Broadway, White Plains, New York 10601. Tel: 1 888 382 7245. www.eurovacations.com*

Senior citizens

Reduced admission is available at most museums. The *Carte Vermeille*, sold at railway stations, gives reduced fares on public transport.

Student and youth travel

More than 25 per cent of visitors to France are under the age of 26. A whole range of special services and facilities exists for this influential group.

The *Carte Jeune* (Youth Card) entitles holders – who must be under 26 – to discounts on public transport, museum admissions, entertainments, shopping and other facilities (including meals at university canteens). The card is available from many outlets. Get details at tourist or post offices, or contact the following:

Centre d'Information et Documentation Jeunesse (National Youth Information and Documentation Centre), *101 quai Branly, 75015 Paris; tel: 08 25 09 06 30; www.cidj.com.*
For the **Fédération Unie des Auberges de Jeunesse** (Youth hostel association), *tel: 01 44 89 87 27.*

There are special fares for under-26s on SNCF. Contact the Rail Shop for information (*see 'By rail' above*).

Sustainable tourism

Thomas Cook is a strong advocate of ethical and fairly traded tourism and believes that the travel experience should be as good for the places visited as it is for the people who visit them. That's why we firmly support The Travel Foundation, a charity that develops solutions to help improve and protect holiday destinations, their environment, traditions and culture. To find out what you can do to make a positive difference to the places you travel to and the people who live there, please visit *www.thetravelfoundation.org.uk*

Telephones

Coin-operated phone booths are no longer common and the *télécarte* phone card has taken over. Buy one in a post office or *tabac* (tobacconist). The cards are much cheaper than a hotel call.

Many phones now accept credit cards too. Cheap rates operate after 8pm and all day Sunday. French telephone numbers have ten digits, of which the first two indicate the region: Paris and the Île de France *01*, the northwest *02*, the northeast *03*, the southeast including Corsica *04*, the southwest *05*.

To make an international call from France, dial *00*, then the country code: **Australia** *61*, **Canada** *1*, **Ireland** *353*, **New Zealand** *64*, **UK** *44*, **USA** *1*. For international directory enquiries dial *3212*.

Time

France is always one hour ahead of the UK and Ireland. It is six to nine hours ahead of the USA, five to nine hours ahead of Canada, seven to nine hours behind Australia and 11 hours behind New Zealand.

Tipping

In restaurants and cafés, service is included in the bill but you might want to leave some small change. Taxi drivers should be tipped 10–15 per cent of the amount on the meter. In hotels, tip porters €1–2 for every item of baggage and chambermaids about €2 a day. Cloakroom attendants in theatres and restaurants should be tipped about €1 per item, toilet attendants 50c, and guides at museums and historic monuments about €1. A 10 per cent tip should be given to hairdressers.

Toilets

There are public toilets at stations, in public buildings and in department stores. In the smaller towns, there may be just one toilet to be shared by both men (*hommes* or *messieurs)* and women (*dames*).

Tourist offices

For information on Provence, contact your local French Government Tourist Office or check *www.franceguide.com*

Australia

Level 13, 25 Bligh Street, Sydney, NSW 2000. Tel: 292 315 244.

Canada
Headquarters *1981 Avenue McGill College, Suite 490, Montréal, QUE H3A 2W9. Tel: (514) 288 2026.*
Ireland
35 Lower Abbey Street, Dublin 1. Tel: 1560 235 235.
UK
Atout France, Lincoln House, 300 High Holborn, London WC1V 7JH. Tel: 09068 244123.
USA
Headquarters *444 Madison Avenue, 10022 New York. Tel: 1514 288 1904.*
Midwest *875 N Michigan Avenue, Chicago, Illinois 60611. Tel: 312 751 7800.*
West Coast *9454 Wilshire Boulevard, Beverly Hills, Los Angeles, CA 90212. Tel: 410 286 8310.*
The regional tourist board is:
Comité Régional de Tourisme
Provence-Alpes-Côte d'Azur, BP4621–F13567, Marseille. Tel: 04 91 56 47 00.
www.decouverte-paca.fr
You could also try these websites:
www.alpes-haute-provence.com;
www.guideriviera.com;
www.visitprovence.com; *www.hautes-alpes.net*; *www.tourismevar.com*;
www.provenceguide.com
When in France, use the local network of tourist information offices – the Office de Tourisme or Syndicat d'Initiative – located in most towns and many villages.

Travellers with disabilities

In recent times, more efforts have been made to welcome travellers with disabilities. In addition to providing better on-the-ground facilities, individual resorts and areas produce publications that give information on accommodation, transport, recreational activities, access to monuments, museums, theatres, etc.

For more information, contact:
Association des Paralysés
Délégation de Paris, 13 Place de Rungis, 75013 Paris. Tel: 01 53 80 92 97.
www.apf.asso.fr
Centre Technique National d'Études et Recherches sur le Handicap
236 bis rue de Tolbaic, Paris 75013. Tel: 01 45 65 59 00.
In Britain, contact: **Atout France**
300 High Holborn, London WC1V 7JH. Tel: 090 6824 4123. www.franceguide.com
A factsheet on France is available from the **Holiday Care Service**, *The Hawkins Suite, Enham Place, Enham Alamein, Andover SP11 6JS. Tel: 0845 124 9971. www.holidaycare.org.uk*
The *AA Guide for the Disabled Traveller* is another helpful publication.

Visas

Those allowed to enter France without a visa (for stays of up to 90 days) include citizens from EU countries, the USA, Canada and New Zealand. All categories of travellers, except holders of a National Identity Card, must be in possession of a valid passport.

Travellers from South Africa will need a visa. People requiring visas should get them in their country of residence. For further visa information check:
www.diplomatie.gouv.fr

Index